Weep
No More

By the same author

Fiction
A YOUNG GIRL'S TOUCH
BORN LOSERS
A LOVE MATCH

Non-fiction
TEARS BEFORE BEDTIME

Weep No More

Barbara Skelton

HAMISH HAMILTON
LONDON

To Bernard and Claudine

HAMISH HAMILTON LTD

Published by the Penguin Group
27 Wrights Lane, London W8 5TZ, England
Viking Penguin Inc., 40 West 23rd Street, New York, New York 10010, USA
Penguin Books Australia Ltd, Ringwood, Victoria, Australia
Penguin Books Canada Ltd, 2801 John Street, Markham, Ontario, Canada L3R 1B4
Penguin Books (NZ) Ltd, 182–190 Wairau Road, Auckland 10, New Zealand

Penguin Books Ltd, Registered Offices: Harmondsworth, Middlesex, England

First published in Great Britain by Hamish Hamilton Ltd 1989

Copyright © Barbara Skelton, 1989

Filmset in Linotron Palatino

Printed in Great Britain by Richard Clay Ltd, Bungay, Suffolk

A CIP catalogue record for this book is available from the British Library

ISBN 0-241-122007

Contents

List of Illustrations

All pictures are reproduced by courtesy of the author.

Chapter I

Weidenfeld

In the early Fifties, a letter arrived from King Farouk to say:

> Dear Kiwi,
>
> Please keep in touch with me so that we can arrange a meeting some time . . .
> and don't dare pass through Italy without dropping in to see me at the
> Villa Dusmet. Otto von Frank.
>
> PS Address your letters in my correct name as usual, please.

When George Weidenfeld invited Cyril to join him on a European culture
tour, I arranged to go to Rome and stay with the deposed King who, after the
abdication, had taken the title of Prince Farouk Fuad. He was living with a
Neapolitan girl in the Grottaferrata area and no longer had a retinue of
servants. It was not a particularly gay interlude. By then, I must have been
considered part of the family, so that when Farouk set off on his nightly
rounds, I would be left behind in the kitchen to keep his mistress Irma
company. She was a buxom, simple, friendly girl, but all she wanted to talk
about were her dreams of becoming a filmstar. Late in the afternoon I would
come upon Farouk eating grilled meat in a pitch-dark alcove. He was supposed
to be on a *régime* and ate kosher butter with his bread. No more jolly jokes and
laughter. He had become a lonely, sagging figure, ostracised by Roman
society, not because of his lax morals, oddly enough – according to Princess
Anne-Marie Aldobrandini, born Anne-Marie Lacloche, daughter of Countess
Volpi, a Venetian lady who had married into Roman society – but because
they found him boring. When she told me this, I expressed surprise. For, many

1

years back, while in Rome with Rex Harrison's first wife, Collette, I met some aristocratic families and, although they lived in enviably beautiful apartments, they were totally devoid of conversation. And *ouf!* were they boring. Like Irma, impoverished Roman gentlemen also had their dreams, not of becoming filmstars but of marrying American heiresses.

In Rome, Farouk was just as quirky as he had ever been. On my departure, he did what I wish I had the courage to do when any book-worms depart; he checked on the contents of my suitcase and came upon a comb belonging to the apartment, which he quickly claimed back. I was about to descend to a taxi waiting to take me to the station, when he called me back and said, 'You've forgotten something,' and my last vision of him was standing in the doorway, with his familiar mocking smile, holding up my toothbrush.

During my visit I received a letter from hubby in Bayreuth, saying,

Darling Baby,

I am sorry for not writing before, it has been so hot, a permanent heat wave in which one is always on the run or else at the opera which one has to attend in a dinner jacket at four pm every roasting afternoon, when one is craving a naked siesta after the morning's sightseeing. My article has to be written between seven and nine am. I am very glad to have seen this but I shall not wish to see it again. An interminable wallow in German pre-Raphaelite folklore, with marvellous moments but vast tracts where, not knowing a word of German except for what the mailbag requires, one sits gazing at fat women berating each other while the mind wanders further and further away and the bottom itches on the hard seat. However, I have learnt *The Ring* and all its good and subtle moments, especially the marvellous orchestral preludes and the general-sense-of-doom themes. It is the last and perhaps the greatest explosion of Romanticism. It is now eight am and more sweltering than ever. I motor in a couple of hours to Munich with W. and Podbielski. Then W. and I take the train to Salzburg where we 'do' another festival. Everyone is beginning to get on my nerves though G.W. has been very charming and tactful and very useful as an interpreter. He chases women and gets more and more Central European, which suits him, a chuff-like, big businessman with wanton, bloodshot eyes and a bulging behind, always in a telephone booth, but there is the domed forehead and considerable intelligence and a soft spot for yours truly, whose fortune he proposes to make.

I managed to get through the operas without being turned out for interruptions and confine 'How's about another million?' and 'Clever little darling baby' (for that is what you are) to the streets, museums and other private places. I miss you very much except when I'm alone, when I feel with you. I long to hear if the handbag arrived and if all is well. My telepathic system tells me that you are sometimes bored and miss your Pop but that on the whole you are enjoying yourself. If we are to meet in Paris, we had better make it the Pont Royal. I don't know if the French strikers will make my Vienna job impossible. I hope to find a word from you in Munich today. Will write again and wire from time to time. All my love, Cyril.

PS There is no happiness outside one's prose. One must create in it the warmth and grace that one doesn't find outside . . .

It was after this cultural jaunt that Cyril changed publishers. He abandoned Hamish Hamilton and got taken on by Weidenfeld.

Of the two categories of individual, the 'present-giver' or 'non-giver', I am inclined to belong to the latter group. My sister Brenda and I were brought up simply to consider presents a waste of money. As a young girl, while modelling at Stiebel's,* I made friends with another model who, thinking I looked lost and lonely, arranged for me to spend my summer holiday as a paying lodger with her aunt in Eastbourne, where I knew no one. In an effort to fill in my day, I answered an advertisement for tuition in ballroom dancing. The instructor turned out to be a white-haired pederast. The lessons consisted in our gliding round an empty room overlooking the seafront, to the accompaniment of a foxtrot or a tango on the gramophone. Soon after this dismal holiday, my friend announced her forthcoming marriage. At a loss to know what to present her with, I dug out of the cupboard a pair of trite blue Venetian candlesticks and I don't think we saw each other again.

Cyril loved giving presents. He would hand them over to you beaming. It might be an exquisite pair of apple-green, leaf-shaped Sèvres fruitbowls that I treasured for years, or Baudelaire's *Les Fleurs du Mal* in a second-hand 1890 edition he had dug out of an Honfleur bookshop and inscribed 'Barbara from Cyril — *séduisants climats*', and although I then hardly understood a verse, the poems were taken to our favourite Normandy beach every day. He inscribed a revised edition of *The Unquiet Grave*:

To beloved brilliant Barbara from Palinurus, Navigator of Silences.

---

* Victor Stiebel was a famous couturier.

'Dry again?' said the crab to the Rock Pool
La Noche Buena 1949 London

This was followed by *Enemies of Promise* and *The Condemned Playground: Essays 1927–1944*.
And then, a re-edition of *The Rock Pool*:

Barbara from Cyril
who knows her
Cagnes

Finally, only two of Cyril's books ever got published by Weidenfeld; the first, *Ideas and Places*:

Barbara from Cyril –
'Let not th' insulting foe my fame pursue
But shade those laurels which descend on you'
May 1953

Second, the *Golden Horizon* of long short stories:

Barbara from Cyril
illam oportet crescere
me autem
minui at her cottage of Elmstead Nov 1953

The following summer, we went to stay with Maurice Bowra in Oxford and while there were driven over to The Close, Bloxham, to lunch with the gourmet, André Simon, author of several cookbooks and set before each *invité*'s plate was the following menu:

The Wines

The Fare

Champagne Moët et Chandon 1943
Coronation Cuvée

Melon

Kidney & Mushroom Soup

Amontillado La Riva 'Guadeloupe'
Bottled 1937

4

◇◇◇

That year, when we passed through London, we no longer indulged in a room at the Ritz. Cyril stayed at his club. I don't remember whose proposal it had been, but I spent the night in the spare room of the new publisher's house in Chester Square. This was after Weidenfeld's wife had left him and his attic quarters had been rented to a Count. Then, one day, Cyril confessed he had become infatuated with Caroline Freud and had been for some time.

'In that case,' I said, 'I shall have to find somebody.' Using the very words of my mother, Cyril replied,

'So long as he is a gentleman, I won't mind.'

'Whom do you consider a gentleman? Weidenfeld?'

'Too continental. But, so far as a continental Jew can be a gentleman, he fits. And . . .,' Cyril added, 'I would prefer him to most people.'

It was about this time that I finished writing *A Young Girl's Touch*. The title had been taken from a calypso, although Rose Macaulay later, perhaps rightly, suggested it should have been entitled *From Kensington to Cairo*. When the manuscript came back from the typist, Weidenfeld perked up interest. He read it and agreed to publish the book. A contract was drawn up and *A Young Girl's Touch* was included in his spring catalogue. Some others on the list were *The Bubblemakers*, *A Legacy* by Sybille Bedford and Marcel Proust's *Jean Santeuil*.

The novel being off my hands, it left a gap in my life. I felt restless, became the avid London-goer and got taken to wallow in German pre-Raphaelite folklore. I don't know whether it was the circumstances in which I first heard it (holding hands with this promising new publisher throughout the many performances of *The Ring*) but Wagner became one of my favourite composers and from then on, whenever I heard the Rhinemaidens, I visualised a chorus of Sonia Orwells.

When, with conflicting feelings of guilt, fret and shame, I admitted to being in love with his publisher, Cyril talked less of Caroline, saying, 'I realised it was making you unhappy,' and, no doubt knowing it would lead to further frustrations, he gave up seeing her and I, not wishing to disrupt our marriage, did everything I could to break the Weidenfeld stranglehold. But W. was very tenacious. Whenever I refused to see him, he elicited sympathy and support from Feliks Topolski or John Sutro, maintaining he was rescuing me from an unhappy marriage, until I eventually relented and agreed to a meeting.

Chapter II

Obsessed

There was an old hag in a hovel.
Who spent her days writing a novel.
When one page was writ
She looked for some shit
And scooped it all up on a shovel.

Diary

Latest development is that Cyril is cross because I have become the avid London-goer. Says he doesn't want to leave the country this week. Has never made such a statement before, not since I've been married to him. Is talking of taking a holiday abroad. Last night he said,

'I know you think I'm mean.'

'Well, you constantly remind me of the money you spend on me.'

'You're always so ungrateful. Now Caroline I smothered with presents.'

'No wonder you're so overdrawn at the bank.'

Wake up this morning with a feeling almost of liberation. Could I really give up W.? How is it I can be in love with someone whose hands and pallor intrude like flaws or speckles in an otherwise perfect photograph? I have had this feeling before of being able to dispel him from my mind, usually after a visit to London, but it doesn't last. Cyril has become angelic, never a grumpy word. Now professes to love it here, never wants to leave Oak Coffin, is disgusted and bored with London, Joan very dull to be with, nobody he wants to see, he would like to kill W. and it would break his heart if we separated. It would break mine too.

Winter has reared its ugly head. The beech tree has shed most of its leaves, the field opposite is sunny with shiny blades of grass rumpled by the wind. The kettle whistle has just sounded. As the char, Mrs Lea, is away I say to Cyril,

'Is that for the washing up?'

'Yes,' he replies, as though to satisfy me, and adds with a giggle, referring to the tap of the typewriter, 'We try to make an author's life as comfortable as possible.' He then goes into the kitchen and proceeds to wash the dishes. I have had a bad night, could not go to sleep for ages brooding in a fury. I wonder why I think of W. with such resentment when I get down here. All that came in the post, *The Thurber Garland*. We discuss the jokes. I say I don't enjoy the wine joke much – 'It's a naïve domestic Burgundy without any breeding, but I think you'll be amused by its presumption.' Cyril says he prefers his own description – 'A well-fendered little wine.'

We had a day in Folkestone, a mouldy tea, scrambled eggs on margarined toast. A windy main street, potboilers already appearing on the bookstalls for Christmas. Books with large photographs of cats and small, boring prints.

Wake up this morning to hear a steady, gentle drizzle, little pinpricks of sound like something sizzling in the grate. A calm, darkish day, very still, an occasional cock crows, and just outside in the lane the old woman from the bungalow calls out to her goat, 'Billie', and, again, the forlorn cry, 'Billie'.

Last night I went to sleep very early without tablets. Was awoken by Cyril groaning in the next room. 'Poor Cyril', over and over, just loud enough for me to hear. Or 'Poor Baby', several times over. When I called out, 'For goodness' sake, Cyril, do shut up,' he did not reply, but merely went on muttering in a lower tone.

I have been to let the geese out of their patch, which is completely shorn of grass.

'One or two eggs for breakfast?' I ask.

'There's no such thing as one egg, it's like one eye,' said Cyril.

Strained soup before we leave for London. The rain has started anew. I was in a fearful state, haunted by W. Rushing round to his house for ten minutes, I found him thinking of nothing but thermostat fires to heat his sitting room.

And all he could talk about was buying a fridge, as his wife had removed the old one with the rest of the furniture.

Cyril and I lunched with Mark Culme-Seymour and his castanet girl, and then we went on to an afternoon drinking club, the Colony. There was Nina Hamnett looking ghastly, her hair uncombed in wisps all over her head. She had just come out of hospital and had her leg in a splint, and was beckoning and calling to everyone to come and talk to her, but although people heard, they simply turned away. The editor of the *Evening Standard*, Frank Owen, and his concubine, Anna Maclaren, their faces puffy with drinking, he with bags under his eyes, and she very made-up and corpulent. John Raymond, his pale podgy countenance like an oversize bum, and John Minton* very tipsy.

The situation is getting more insoluble and distressing. I find it increasingly difficult to think of leaving Cyril and yet I seem to have inwardly made up my mind to do so. Whenever he talks of the future (some fresh plan to tour Kenya with the Davises) I go dead on him. And yet, when I consider being married to W., it does not seem to be what I want at all. I am simply obsessed with him sexually. I no longer remark on his hands or his toenails. And I have told him that he must grow some more black hair on his back. I have even threatened to smear him with some bone lotion to further the process.

The whole of the lower part of my body aches from the thighs down. It's the humidity, in spite of two blankets and Cyril's mother's hydrax rug spread over the bed. Last night, we drank champagne. Tried to make *blinis* to use up some stale smoked salmon. Cyril whipped the egg whites and rolled the *blinis* round the smoked salmon at the finish. Mrs Lea comes today for the first time in a fortnight.

'She's arrived,' Cyril calls, 'the worst is over.'

The usual banging about in the kitchen and the sound of someone scraping burnt toast. 'When was the happiest time of your life?'

'Oh, I don't know,' I say. 'One always underestimates an experience in retrospect.'

---

* John Raymond wrote a book on Simenon and was, amongst other things, an editor of the *New Statesman*. John Minton, the artist, committed suicide in 1957.

Wake up thinking of W., but am otherwise very content. I should hate to have to give up living here. It is a bright, glistening morning, the sun is shining into my room, the grass tips gleam and quiver in the breeze, beyond a certain distance the field is enveloped in mist which peters out on the skyline into a blob of treetops; occasionally a branch of the beech stirs, but everything else remains still. Cyril has begun to correct his novel, which he refers to as a thriller; it's called *Shade Those Laurels*.

Thursday night we went again to see *Waiting for Godot*, this time with Peter Watson, and enjoyed it even more the second time. On the way into the theatre, I remarked on Peter's overcoat and asked Cyril why he didn't get one like it; it was fur-lined in imitation beaver that covered the lapels and looked as though it were waterproof. Cyril said he thought it was horrible, like a Belgian taximan's coat. Afterwards we dined at the Café Royal Grill. A delicious room, mirrors and painted stucco figures. Peter was seething with malice which came out in giggly innuendoes. I was wearing my fitch-lined coat and when Cyril suggested taking it to the cloakroom, Peter, in a high-pitched, ironical tone, said, 'Oh! Do you think we ought?' (As though I'd been worried about losing such a precious object.) When I explained that I didn't like it anyway, he thought I was being affected. I still think he's the most delightful of Cyril's friends, although now he has become rather slouchy and shrivelled with a bitter glint in his eye. He made fun of me for liking the painter John Bratby and later, when Cyril was referring to a Tissot in the Proust exhibition which I failed to remember, Peter said, 'I don't expect it was realistic enough for her,' and screeched with laughter as if he'd said the funniest thing. Seeing I was put out, as I couldn't see why it was that funny, he thought I was piqued and, leaning forward, wiped the front of my pullover free of bread crumbs with an affectionate flick, as though to make up for his quip. He said he thought *L'Oeil* was a terribly good magazine and how ghastly he found London. I reminded them of how three years ago at the Ritz we had all said how much we hated London and yet there was Peter settling into a new flat. We spent the night at Sonia's. It was quite cosy really, although I kept saying it was like a dreary middle-class secretary's abode with its terrible oak, let-down leaf table, the soiled blue eiderdown, and tasteless carpets and curtains. Before getting into the bucket bed, I said to Cyril, 'What about pulling the curtains?' and he chanted, 'When the how's-about-it start, block your ears and loose a fart.'

Have just read corrected part of Cyril's novel; he has another hundred pages to do. It is getting much better, but I feel the dinner party goes on too long, perhaps because I have read it before. I feel it should be much better and hoped that after his corrections I would be more stimulated. It is wonderful that he does it at all; I keep asking to read what he has done, hoping to give him encouragement. There has been talk of our going to Sardinia. Cyril bought a guide which says, 'Sardinian cuisine is simple and pleasing like the people,' and includes some specialities:

Succa Tundu or *Fregula*: a thick meat soup made with semolina.
Buttariga: dried eggs from mullets.
La Cauladda: cauliflower soup.
Cordula: lamb bowels on the spit.
Giogga Minudda: boiled snails.

'Those that don't sound alarming just seem dull,' Cyril remarked and went up to bed.

We have just had John Russell to stay. This morning he rang up to say that the visit had tipped him over into the New Year in capital spirits . . . he thanked us for putting up so nicely with his dullness. His silence, he said, had been a philosophical one in which he saw himself transported into a simple dwelling of some nineteenth-century emigrant. A disciple of Coleridge, blissfully marooned in the *new found land* with his dream consort. A life of study, meditation, wholesome fare and early nights with an unspoiled queen of the jungle; we were to take care not to invite him again because he would immediately accept and we would be most welcome at Palazzo Percy* that had fallen into a truly Victorian state of dilapidation.

Telephone rings at midnight and Cyril gets to it before I am fully awake. It was clearly W., who hung up on Cyril. The result was that Cyril had a bad night. Says he cannot work on his novel if I am going to upset him like that and muttered all night, 'Poor Cyril'. In the morning I go into his room in search of matches and would like to give him a kiss, but think that by doing so it is giving him too much encouragement. Wrote to W., to say that telephoning was a mistake, asking him not to do it again.

---

* Poppet John, who was then married to a Dutch painter, Pol, had rented her flat in Percy Street to John Russell.

We have just got back from London after giving Maugham, Alan Searle and Angus Wilson lunch. I arrived in the nick of time, having had a secret meeting with W., in a pub round the corner. He was looking very much less attractive this week; the week before, when I met him after seeing the jumper woman, he appeared to be much slimmer and glamorous even, wearing a new grey overcoat and, with his alert stride and bright brown eyes – compared by some evil tongues to iron jelloids – I felt terribly in love. We went to Overton's and ate sandwiches. It was only when he broke the news that the following week he could not keep his luncheon date with me as he had to go to some *boring* bachelor anniversary given by Ben Nicolson that some of the charm wore off.

At lunch, Maugham said that at his age one could look back on most promising writers of his youth who might just as well never have written a word.

Cyril had ordered a special piece of beef but everyone complained about loss of appetite. Alan said he suffered from liver trouble and could not eat meat. I have noticed that at every meal we've had with them he always has to consult Maugham before he can decide what he should eat. When I asked whom he had most enjoyed seeing this time in London, Alan said an old friend of his called Anna May Wong, one of his early romances. Alan hated *Waiting for Godot*; the tramps' dirty feet worried him and he couldn't see the point of the small boy, or angel, as we saw him. Maugham said he had enjoyed it because the second act had been up to standard and it was always the most difficult part of a play to do. Angus Wilson said he couldn't like any play with tramps in it; he didn't like the idea of people being wanderers who didn't settle down in life. His play, *The Mulberry Bush*, on the other hand, was very good. Maugham advised him to go to rehearsals as often as he could. It was very important to get the feel of a play and it helped one to make improvements. Maugham praised the *cœur de filet de bœuf*, it was so delicious and tender. I always like seeing Alan Searle and Maugham. I find them restful, modest and well-mannered.

Not only does Cyril already have a genet (a kind of civet) costing £20 in the care of Mr Flewin at the zoo, but he has also persuaded the *Sunday Times* to buy him a lemur from Harrods in exchange for an article on them. The lemur has enchanting ways, purrs when stroked or petted, woofs when fretful, swings from the branches, romps like a kitten, but the worst horror, it is a relentless destroyer of buds and leaves, and when trapped in the cat basket, springs up and down on its forepaws, in a caged, neurotic fashion, banging its head on the top of the basket. He has named her Wirra. She is the *Sunday Times* mascot, totally dependent on human beings and a source of non-stop worry.

I am having book-jacket trouble. The painter, Eleanour Bellingham-Smith, was hopeless, she did a cover of herself at the age of twelve; Mosley is vulgar; so, in the end. Cyril rang up Leonard Rosoman.

Chapter III

In Hospital

Peter Watson died last week. He was found dead in his bath. It is not known yet what was the cause. Cyril and Stephen Spender obituary-conscious. Cyril's more moving but hopelessly cut in the 'Atticus' column:

> Mr Peter Watson, who died unexpectedly at the age of forty-nine, held a unique place in the world of modern art. As a young man he stepped, gay and delightful, out of a charmed existence like a Mayfair Buddha suddenly sobered by the tragedy of his time to become the most intelligent, generous and discreet of patrons, the most creative of connoisseurs, the possessor of a formative flair which sought out everything that was contemporary, international and alive in painting and music. He founded and financed the magazine *Horizon*, of which he was the art editor from 1939 to 1950, and became one of the four founders of the Institute of Contemporary Arts.

At this stage of our marital stress, encouraged by Cyril who had always wanted me to have a child, I consulted a gynaecologist. It was not the first attempt. Previously I had been told that before being given treatment, I would have to undergo an operation for the removal of some fibroids, which I decided to do and a lady surgeon booked me into Canterbury Hospital.

The day before going into hospital, Cyril greeted me at Charing Cross with the words, 'Well, at any rate, I have some good news. Mary Campbell knows all about fibroids. When her cows get them they become so randy they're good for nothing and have to be shot!'

We spent the night before in Canterbury at the Abbot's Barton Hotel. Our room had a large window looking on to grass bordered by a neatly trimmed beech hedge. Both with healthy appetites, we dined in the hotel on boiled ham. The following morning, we took a taxi to the hospital. Cyril sat next to the driver. I found his back view very touching, the uncombed hair round a bald patch on the pudding basin head, his coat collar crumpled inward and, when he turned towards me, his pale blue eyes had the pained expression of an injured child, not knowing what he had done to deserve such punishment. He stayed with me all day, merely disappearing for an hour in the afternoon to buy a cyclamen in a pot and six yellow roses, and got back to find I had already received a dozen red ones. Yes! He had wanted to be the first person to give me flowers, so I said, 'They're only from Chuff,' adding that I preferred his yellow roses and the fact that there only six make them more touching. He must have a kiss for them. He gives a deep sigh and says, 'Ahhhh', on a low note of pain. W. is talked about all the rest of the day: if I went to live with him, how he would always be unfaithful; how Jews get so unattractive in middle age. I am given a blood test; am shaved. The anaesthetist plops all over my breast. A nurse tests my breathing and in between Cyril goes on running down W. Describes Sutro and W. as bubble-blowing babies who expect everyone to gather round and watch them fart. Compares our situation to *Carmen*, only, instead of a matador, the lover is a Jewish businessman.

The surgeon, a provincial drill-mistress in her early thirties, comes in for a final interview. She states the swelling is in a very difficult position and it might be necessary to remove the womb altogether.

'Are you in agreement?'

'Definitely not,' I say. What one had thought was going to be a simple operation suddenly turns out to be a nightmare. 'If I can't have a child,' I say to Cyril, 'I shall feel utterly useless to everyone.' C. just sits beside the bed and glares. As he was unable to cheer me up, I begged him to leave. 'You make me feel worse sitting there glaring,' I say.

Cyril has just been to see me; he brought Wirra with him. She is a changed animal, hibernating and affectionate, with hanging breasts. I compared her changed aspect to our old char, Mrs Munro, and said one couldn't think of her as being pretty any more after seeing that rump. Advised him to sell her before she incurred even more expense to zookeepers to look after her, otherwise he would spend the rest of his life carrying that smelly little basket around. Cyril asked if I had made a will.

'You must write on a slip of paper that you leave the cottage and everything in it to me, it's the least you can do.'

'What about my ice?' (the Boucheron clip that Farouk had given me out of his winnings in La Baule casino).

'I don't care about that.' As he had been seeing a lot of Elaine Dundy, authoress of *The Dud Avocado*, I said, 'You could always give it to Elaine Tynan.'

'No, I wouldn't do that.'

'Or pin it on to Wirra's rump.'

'You're in a good humour,' Cyril said peevishly.

The ward sister has just been in and said, 'We'll be moving you after lunch, when you get back from theatre.' Nurses very sweet and attentive. Begin to think it an ideal life, lying in bed with the sound of voices and a hoover in the distance. Am very tired after a succession of bad nights in London, quarrels and crises. Compare my feelings of a year ago with today, relatively content; imagine I could be separated from W., to lead my own life without much regret. Situation with Cyril remains bad. He is invariably in a bad humour, when his expression conveys permanent disgust, a cross between an angry rodent and a beaver. Always this great insistence on knowing the truth. 'I am an intellectual and must hear the truth.' And then, when he gets it, he collapses. When I said to him, 'To think how wretched I was a year ago and now am relatively content. I could never be as much in love again,' he said, 'You mean to say you were in love with him?'

'What do you think all the fuss was about, then?'

Cyril has just telephoned. Very *doux* for a change. When I told him that this was the life for me — lying in bed with the sound of food trays being prepared along the passage, newspapers brought in in the morning, soliciting people who come in, quiet reading, an occasional guest, early nights, and a pleasant view of trees and grass from the window — Cyril said, 'We must see about getting you into a psychiatric ward next time!'

Cables pour in, sometimes three a day. Greetings telegrams with cupids blowing trumpets, horseshoes, roses and blue violins, wishing me luck and sending infinite love, asking me to telephone, and ending up with affection and more love, George. Then came a telegram with felicitations on the operation being successful, he was hurrying up the proofs of my book, I was to resist being influenced by any distorted tittle-tattle, he was longing for the weekend, he would telephone, in the meantime he awaited a letter and hoped it would be friendly. Then, later in the day, another message came saying I was to believe in our happiness together in spite of everything ... he had telephoned three times and how frustrated he felt because I had not gone to the telephone or sent back any messages, but he was coming to the hospital on Saturday and Sunday, I was to tell the nurse what I wanted him to bring and recommend a hotel in Canterbury, he was thinking of me incessantly and desperately, lovingly, George. So I wrote:

Nurse very amused that you expected me to get to the telephone this morning. I am immovable even in bed and was drugged. Had nine little fibroids removed and one big one blocking the tubes. The flowers have been much admired by each nurse in turn. I gave sister some as there were so many; she was very pleased. Will get her to book a room for you in the town and expect to see you two-thirty Saturday. That's the visiting hour. Hope you are not fretting but keeping your mind on business. The roses have been much admired again. 'You are very spoilt,' one of the nurses said. Very sleepy, love . . .

The following day he said he was constantly dreaming of a Roman December and Sicily for Christmas, and incessantly thinking of and awaiting Saturday. He had caught himself doodling with breadcrumbs throughout an entire French Embassy dinner, forming the first five letters of my name; he felt wildly frustrated and was impatiently awaiting our reunion, he would be arriving in Canterbury early morning, he would telephone . . .

The next letter conveyed he was anguished at telephone difficulties . . . he was going to try again in the evening, he hoped all his telegrams would have reached me by tonight, sincerest love and devotion unreserved . . .

The following day he was begging me to ring at two-thirty even if it was just for one minute or maybe try just for two seconds around seven . . .

He had had a long talk with Feliks most affectionately about me, he was so sorry to have been out when I called but he had been chasing after *The Noble Savage*, a life of Paul Gauguin, he was thinking of me constantly and counting time until Saturday and sent more floods of love . . .

Thought I was going to enjoy being in a private room, but the day drags. Though I do at last have a book which keeps me absorbed, *Lord Byron's Marriage* by G. Wilson Knight. Even so, one can read only for so long, seven hours it has been, and then one's head reels. With this operation there is no treatment during the day, which takes up the time. Night nurses come in at six-thirty just when one is awake, take temperature, bring toothmug and bowl of hot water to wash hands and then buzz off. Day nurses come on and make the bed, the cleaner arrives and sweeps, breakfast, the newspapers (read about Bodkin Adams case*), then what they call 'a blanket bath', which means I strip and wash myself. No sun today. Was given two pain-killing tablets this morning which are beginning to wear off. Cyril telephones and says he enjoyed his dinner with the Hamish Hamiltons, Stephen Spender, the Ian Gilmours and Mark Longman; thought an extra woman would have helped. Got a lot of attention from Gilmour and Longman who monopolised Cyril throughout dinner in order to make Jamie feel 'socially inadequate'. I said, 'How childish.' C. agreed it was cliquey. He said that if I marry W. it will last a year. After that he will be in constant touch with his lawyers.

W. telephoned, full of groans. The new servant, Phillips, no good, not doing any work, can't cook, how he misses the Italian Enzo (his Leporello) who is on holiday, has Lizzy Lezard coming for lunch. Originally, he promised to come to Canterbury for the weekend; now states a Mr Blow has come from America with whom he will have to spend Friday evening and he also has to see his child. I tell him not to bother and arrange for Cyril to come instead. Cyril says he will come for the whole of Saturday, stay the night. In the end, turns up on Sunday. Not much to choose between them, really.

Cyril went to Brussels the weekend I came out of hospital and Sutro sent a car for me. I was booked into the Westbury, where W. had taken a room. When Cyril got back he also moved into the hotel, from where he wrote to the Bill Davises:

---

* Dr Adams practised in Eastbourne. He was then on trial for murdering a wealthy widow by administering large quantities of drugs. In her will she had bequeathed him a chest full of silver. Adams was eventually acquitted. The writer Sybille Bedford attended the trial and described it in her book, *The Best We Can Do*.

Barbara wants to get away from the ding-dong to rest and try to make up her mind. She was about to go to Poppet's when vexation at W. (alas only temporary), as she wanted him to hand over evidence for a divorce to my lawyer, made her decide to go to you. Naturally, I am delighted because (a) she is with you (b) she is somewhere where he can't telephone her . . . but it does mean that she is really with me . . . or even really trying to give him up. I suppose she will try to see whom she misses most – if it is me she will send for me and I shall fly out, if it is him, I suppose she will leave you. If I join her we would stay with you a long time and do the short book on Spain I have to do – for which she must learn to do colour photographs. Of course, I long to come for Christmas, but not if it is going to drive her away. And I want you to be very tactful and not root for me too obviously but make her feel you both like her for herself as I know you do . . . she has had a very bad time between the operation and the wear and tear of trying to have two husbands simultaneously. I can only say that she means to get over him and stay with me . . . but is also inclined to think she is bad for me. She suffers a lot of guilt when with him. Perhaps you could introduce her to the bullfighter Litri or some other distraction. A trip to Tangier or Marbella would also be welcome but try to keep that for when I come . . . don't let her get depressed in the evenings, it is when she missed W. at the cottage, but run her down to Toni's bar. I have been through hell the last weeks and it is an immense relief that she is going away and not always on the floor below here seeing us both alternately. Have had very bad time. Very much love from Cyril . . .

Chapter IV

In Spain

Diary

Churriana

The airport of Gibraltar is as beautiful as Nice's. The plane coasted in very slowly and landed on a long strip jutting out into the sea. One was suddenly engulfed by the land and ships, and when the engines were turned off, I felt as though I'd been swallowed up into nothingness. Bill was nowhere to be seen and I began to get depressed, thinking my telegram had not arrived in time. I was about to leave and book into the Rock Hotel when I saw them unloading parcels, all bent over the boot of a large grey sportscar: Bill, Annie and her brother, Tom Bakewell, a handsome playboy who has opened a bar in Torremolinos. They had spent the day in Gibraltar and been stocking up, and were so friendly and seemed so pleased to see me that I immediately felt happy that I'd come. But the drive was terribly tiring as it was fiesta; the streets were crowded with horses, donkeys and Spaniards strolling up and down in their best and brightest clothes. We drank Scotch all the way and Bill was interested to hear about the operation; if I had a scar, what shape was it and which way did it run?

'No intercourse from the day I came out of hospital for six weeks,' I told him, knowing it was the kind of detail he relished, and with great seriousness he worked out the dates. He is a very funny man. When we arrived at La Consula, we drank a lot more Scotch on the rocks, played negro spirituals on the gramophone and lit all the big log fires.

It's so wonderful to be here, in this well-run atmosphere of calm, luxury and quiet, apart from the baying of watchdogs at night, the wailing of nine

Siamese cats and a turkey that chortles in the early morning. The house is very beautiful; white-faced with a line of columns. One enters through high iron gates with a vista of a gravel drive, a line of columns on one side and a dense, wooded, tropical garden on the other – very romantic at night. Everything is modern and white. They have some very good Giacomettis and some Goya prints; there are log fires in all the rooms, the dining room is lit by candles and the meat cooked on a charcoal grill. Bill is a great expert on food and chases after the servants so that everything is properly served. They have two horses in the paddock. If only I felt well enough to ride.

A lot of confidences were shared while we sat over the dying embers of the charcoal grill. Bill said that I felt for Cyril pretty much as he had felt for his first wife, whom he'd lost 'for a good lay'.

'Now, if you leave Cirrule, what has this fellow got to offer you?'

'Well, he hasn't got anything, really, Bill.'

'The way I see it, this fellow'll get on. I like his books. See! I should say that in about fifteen years he'll be rich. But what's the good of that to you, Baubra?'

'No good at all, Bill.'

'I'm not sure you wouldn't do better to stay as you are and keep writing. You never know, you might have some luck. If Cirrule says you could be good you will be. He wouldn't say anyone was good if he didn't believe it.'

'It's gone too far for that, Bill,' interrupts Annie, 'she's got to decide between them.'

'Are you in love with him?'

'I suppose I am, Bill.'

'Well, Baubra, if he gives you enough *meat*, it might work out. But you should get him to give you some shares in the business.'

I suppose I find them endearing and funny because of their low, drawling, Yankee accents.

Woke up this morning with a fearful sore throat and the usual sensation of pending disaster. My breakfast was brought in on a basket tray that just fitted over the knees with pockets either side for books and newspapers. In my bedroom everything is also white with thick cedarwood doors and shutters, a marble floor with honey-coloured matting and a view of palms. Last night the Brenans came to dinner, the usual cattiness about people – very reminiscent of England. Pritchett got it this time, but everything Gerald Brenan said about Spain was amusing and interesting. I shall go and sit in the sun on the terrace before a lovely view of the sea and mountains. One feels too hot in a pullover, the sun is so strong, but once it's gone down around four o'clock, the temperature seems to be freezing.

The first twenty-four hours of euphoria at being out of London in an atmosphere of calm and luxury has now subsided and I suffer from mild melancholia; between six and eight it gets worse, and at the very mention of Robin and Mary Campbell my dread sinks to its lowest level. The royal suite is being prepared and they are talked of with bated breath as being very *special* people.

I wrote to darling Cyril:

> It's a very *triste* evening, gusty, grey and chilling. My room is rather cold and I miss my red dressing gown more than anything. There are three Siamese cats that roam the house yowelling; the males have black, furry balls to match their ears. They all sprawl over each other making the same sex-mad noise as our stray cat last winter. Annie is being exceptionally forthcoming in her efforts to cheer me up, talks of possible future trips, but the only reaction from Bill is a frown as he stretches out his legs and yawns. I think he is bored with this house. He spends all his time taking short walks round the garden, carrying a cane, dressed like an English squire and playing the gramophone, or darting in and out of Malaga. He doesn't seem in the least interested in the children and never addresses a word to them. I have only seen Annie's brother, Tom, and his wife once. She is extremely pretty like a young Gerda, surprisingly lacking in vanity and more intelligent than him.
>
> The Gate House [where Cyril hoped we would live while he did a short book on Spain] is half the size of the cottage, comfortable and pokey, with no view and very dark – perfectly good for a lone author in a working mood or for two blissfully happy midgets. Gerald asked after you and said you were one of the few writers who was not envious of other writers. The Campbells have arrived, they improve things up to a point. But I don't know why, I still find them intermittently provoking. I like Annie the best of the lot, she's a really good, kind person, probably saved from being spoilt through Bill controlling all the money. But with the regular visits of the Brenans, it's like having to stick to a rather indigestible diet of the same food every day. Mary starts putting on long-playing records at nine in the morning (classics, of course) which can be heard all over the house and, except on rare occasions, to me music before luncheon is equivalent to smoking on an empty stomach.
>
> Just received your telegram. I don't know what to say. Don't misinterpret

whatever I wire back. I don't want to make you more unhappy, but the decision to give up W. entirely by going back to you I find impossible to make. If you have not made any plans for Christmas, I think you ought to come here, you will be less gloomy with the Davises than with other people. But now that I'm better, there is a certain monotony about the routine. Bill goes into Malaga each morning so early that one invariably misses him and I don't like suggesting that we go in later. One is as cut off and hermit-like as at the cottage. They never go into Torremolinos and avoid Tommy's bar like the plague. The reason being, Bill says, that he thinks Tom will get into trouble with the police one day, through rival restauranteurs, and he doesn't want to get mixed up in it.

I miss you, of course, but am still bewildered about what to do, as now it has to be a decisive move. Too depressed to pursue the matter. With love, Barbara.

At this stage of our drama many people were involved. In his autobiography Feliks wrote:

My days . . . weeks were stolen by the trio demanding my attention one after the other for the display of their ego-desire remedies. George, the supreme embodiment of the manipulator-errant, assumed to be destined for the highest trophies on account of his steely soullessness, had emerged now at his sexual Grail . . .

Then, there was Sutro and W.'s old friend, Anne Bassett. She had been in touch with me while I was in hospital to say how unhappy George was, that she had known him ever since 1938 when he first came to England at the age of nineteen, that they had worked together in the same department of the BBC and that after the war she had been his private secretary on *Contact*, and that she had never heard him talk about a woman as if she *were* 'a real woman' – as she put it – and he had struck her as being so sincerely devoted that she wanted me to know it, as she was very fond of him and she hoped I wouldn't be angry at her for butting into my private life. Then, at some stage, Mary McCarthy had been drawn into the affair. W. was then her publisher for the English edition of *A Charmed Life* and I remember our meeting, Mary and I, in the bar of the Ritz, when she appeared as W.'s spokeswoman to try and make me come to some decision in his interest, and flashing the smile with which she imparted bad news.

Cyril's devotees were the Davises, Mary and Robin Campbell and my mother. Mail flowed back and forth between Cyril and my Mummy, whose letters were tinged with old-fashioned good sense and disloyalty.

(1)

Dear Cyril,

I was distressed to get your letter today. I was hoping that you were with Barbara. I got a card from her saying that she was still very sore and unable to do much but hoped that the rest and sunshine would do her good. I feel so sorry for you both as I feel that she will never be happy. I can't help thinking that you must have hurt her in some way as she was very much in love with you and was quite happy to settle in the country and live a simple life. I remember last New Year's Eve when she came over to me as she had been left alone in the cottage and she seemed then to be in a very distressed frame of mind. I am afraid you are not suited to each other. She always wants to come first and evidently with this other man she does. I think under it all she has a great homing instinct. I can only hope that all will be well in the end and whatever happens it will be for the happiness of both of you. Yours, Eveline Skelton . . .

(2)

Dear Cyril,

I have not answered your last letter as I have been waiting to hear from B. I wrote to her but had no reply. I was not at all surprised that she told you I did not love her and did not care what she did. She always likes to protect herself but believe me I have gone through just as heart-breaking a time as you are having at the moment . . . there have been times that I have not heard from her for months and sometimes years . . . I did not know of her marriage to you until I read it in the paper . . . that is very hurtful, but I always hope and pray that she will be happy . . . Poor Barbara, I have never known her to be really happy. What does she want? She hates anyone vulgar and loud. I am terribly sorry for you, too; I do hope that your belongings are being looked after at the cottage. You have some beautiful things there and it makes me quite miserable to think of all your books and treasures getting damp. B. always said that you hated the cottage and used to call it Oak Coffin, so perhaps you don't mind very much leaving it. I am

24

afraid I have nothing good or hopeful to tell you but when I get in touch with B., I will let you know. Please call me Evie — that is the name I have always gone by. I hate the sound of mother-in-law. Yours affectionately, Evie . . .

(3)

Dear Cyril,

Thank you for your letters and letting me know the latest developments. I never hear from Barbara unless she is in a fix about something. I cannot understand how you can let her dangle you on a string, so to speak. My advice to you if you think she still loves you is to keep her wondering, do not write to her and let her make the first move. I cannot imagine what this George can be like. My younger daughter, Brenda, said on the phone that he had a very foreign voice, which I should have thought would have put anyone off. However, Barbara is Barbara . . . Evie

(Mummy had, in fact, written soon after our marriage to say, 'I was very thrilled to hear that you were married. You didn't say who to, except Cyril, so do not know how to address you. However, I hope you will both be happy. Tell your husband that you have a mother lurking in the background who would love to meet her son-in-law . . .')

Everyone hoped that the visit to Churriana would prove a turning point in the affair, that there I would come to my senses and from then on the marriage would pick up, which is probably why Bill went into Malaga alone, in order to intercept the mail. One or two pleading cables, however, managed to break the barrier to the effect that he was missing me and I simply must go to our meeting in Madrid . . . he hoped I wouldn't waver, for he simply had to see me. Did I need my overcoat for Christmas? I was to enjoy my rest but not prolong it. Would I please react to his cables? He then put a call through to the village of Churriana to say how depressed he was, as he had deduced from my lack of response that I had decided we could never make a happy marriage. He said he had been promised a small house near Genoa in the spring and summer, but first of all we simply had to meet and discuss everything. So I agreed to fly to Madrid, and a final cable arrived to say that this was going to be a very crucial meeting and, he was sure, wildly exciting and wonderful, with love and *au revoir*.

25

I then wrote to Cyril:

The Campbells have been very kind and sensible. Robin has done his utmost to keep me here, but it is really hopeless. Although I love being here, a quiet life makes me brood. You need to be in a whirl of activity to forget an obsession. I am utterly miserable. If only you could accept my seeing W. from time to time, but you cannot. Whatever happens, I don't want to be married to anyone but you, but if you want a divorce, I will send the evidence, use it if you want to, though I know I shall want to go back to you in the end . . .

A cable arrived saying: 'Darling Barbara if you must go please leave evidence with Robin . . . But entreat you to think again . . . Do grow up and understand about love if you hurt me you will hurt yourself and be unhappy for the rest of your life . . . Merry Christmas Wopsie . . .'

Then I announced my departure for Madrid and Bill took me to the airport. But when I said goodbye and went to embrace him, he shied away. They had taken me under their wing to please Cyril and my departure was considered to be an act of total betrayal. The Davises never forgave me and I was never allowed into La Consula again. When I got to the Hotel Fenix, W. had not arrived due to a plane strike.

But I ran into an old suitor from Queen Street days. Kemali was staying in the hotel with his plump Spanish girlfriend. W. turned up next day and we spent a harmonious Christmas with occasional bouts of gloom on his part. 'What a miserable, ill-fated pair!' 'What are we going to do now?' 'I feel restless and want to benefit from my freedom!' 'I think I need a month to think everything over . . .' 'Suppose I should want another woman! How will you take it?' A harassed expression and cuticle-biting. Then he flew back to England leaving me to pace, groan and brood over his final speech: 'So much has been said or not said that words have become a distrusted currency between us. I don't blame you for feeling deeply disillusioned in me today, for I greatly share your feelings and, more strongly, I feel terrible distress at this convulsive, contortion-like sense of uncertainty I have displayed here. I only want to say this. I love you more than I ever loved anyone else or shall, I think, love anybody. I want you as a person, as a woman, as a wonderful human being and as a wife but I must have a few days of mental peace. Madrid has been both soothing and distressing, very happy and dreadfully sad. I came here in a confused state of mind about our future, partly inflicted by my "conflict", partly persecuted by London propaganda. Please darling,' he said, 'consider that two days ago you yourself suggested a seven-week break followed by a reunion to give me a "taste of freedom"'; but he insisted, 'I do not now want this "taste" – I want merely a breathing space to regain sanity and then for you to join me. I shall prepare the house and the ground for you – symbolically; you will come and be welcomed and received. Yes, darling, I do mean passionately every word I say. It is not a breathing space to "think things over" but just to find myself and be ready to receive you forever! Please do nothing precipitate or impulsive in the next few days. Just answer my telegrams and be available for calls and let me know constantly where you are. Please understand and recover your faith in me.' And off he flew.

Momentary relief while lunching with Kemali and his girlfriend. They talked of a trip of Palma. But optimism soon dissipated. What do I want with these people?! They cannot relieve the depression. It's preferable to be alone.

At seven o'clock – it must have been the time of W.'s arrival in London – came a feeling of complete calm; the storm of misery abated. The crisis was over. I enjoyed my evening with Kemali and thought no more of W.

Sure enough, the following morning I was handed a 'Cable of the Universe', a large, blue globe surrounded by holly and mistletoe. For wasn't it Christmas still? 'URGENT SENORA CONNOLLY Hotel Fenix Madrid'. The cable had been sent from London Airport and he seemed to have had a stormy flight, to be miserable and self-hating; he wanted me to join him on Saturday; on my arrival I would find 'red roses red carpet a breakfast tray Sunday and real honest love'. He seemed distressed because I had refused to accept any telephone calls; I was not to think he was crying wolf when he claimed that his call had been urgent as he was ill. He hoped I had slept well and please would I take his call at nine in the evening?

Later that day, another urgent Cable of the Universe. He had been talking to his mother, had told her everything about us; she had been furious at his veering and hoped as he did that I would fly to London on Saturday.

The third cable marked 'URGENT' conveyed how desperate he was as I refused to accept any calls. I was to forgive him for having a call put through to Kemali's room so late at night, but he had instructed them to try both rooms thinking I might be having a drink with him. He had had a very bad night with injections and he begged me to wire that I would join him on Saturday, and hoped I would accept a call a little later in the day. I wired to say 'Think carefully not hysterically avoiding later regrets missed opportunities me thinking too love Barbara.'

The following day two cables arrived, both apologising for besieging me but he felt physically wretched and collapsed and the doctor had been. I was not to interpret that as pressure on his part but a token of sadness, and would I please accept a morning call and return to London in any mood and on any terms?

Nuit urgente, he had thought carefully and not hysterically. He could not live without me; his only regret would be to lose me forever. He wanted me to marry him and return as begged before in time for the New Year. He had checked with BEA and there was a hundred percent chance of a seat tomorrow. I was to believe that this was his final decision and we were going to start a New Year life together which would give me great scope for artistic and satisfying work by helping him reading and planning books and giving him courage and he remained my ever devoted George.

I flew back to England and settled into Chester Square. Two weeks later I was living alone at the cottage preparing my departure for Morocco and cabling was resumed.

Would I please telephone him before collecting my ticket? He simply had to see me. I had left him feeling quite wretched. And contrary to what I might think, there was still a lot to be said. I was to telephone at once and return to Chester Square.

While at the cottage, I lit a fire one evening, in the sitting room and, cleaning out two built-in cupboards filled with years of junk, one either side of the fireplace, came upon a brown paper bag filled with live cartridges that had been left behind by PC Boot. I don't need these, I thought, flinging them into the flames. Whereupon they exploded and shot all over the room like fireworks, grazing the bridge of my nose and narrowly missing an eye.

When W. managed to get me on the telephone he said, 'I left the Ritz last night feeling more wretched and more contrite than, I think, I shall ever feel. The last fortnight is still vivid in my mind. It is essential that I put to you one or two things quite clearly because whatever you decide to do *please* take note that so much has been said, groaned and hinted between us at Chester Square these last few days that it would be unfair to take isolated snatches of conversation and disregard the others. I *do not* want you to go back to Cyril and I am not afraid of the divorce scandal. I signed my papers as "Co-Respondent" today and whatever happens will happen! I love you and want you. I was caught up in an indissoluble tangle of feelings, conflicts, fears and feverish frets, and lost my balance. *But* the outstanding fact is that I love you and do not want to be with anyone else. In modest self-defence I should like to say that you, too, did not help me in that fortnight, for while you entered the spirit of tragedy completely you did not respond to the intermittent moods of constructiveness. But please believe me that I quite understand all you had to face! In Madrid you said – spontaneously – that a spell of "living on our own" would be good for both of us. If I tell you now that I repent last Thursday and Friday's behaviour and beg you to come back, you may not believe me and, indeed, be more incensed than ever. But I *do* and I feel it. But so that I am given my full share of punishment let me wait a bit but *please* do not commit yourself to a return to C.! I believe that you have emotionally emancipated yourself from him forever. I also believe that much of the bitter experience is due to the pattern of his behaviour and the publicity he gave to every one of his and our moves. I was horrified to hear that you thought *I* was sending other people as emissaries to you or Cyril with the object of fostering your resumption or to save *me* from a divorce scandal. Please, darling, when you are in Morocco, rest and recover, and *please* do not judge too harshly what happened and if you feel so inclined come back to me. By then I should be free and, at any rate, the anomalous and tangled situation of two "unfree" people living together will be reduced to saner proportions.

'I wish to confirm to you that I want you to help me with editorial work. As I explained to you yesterday, it would entail part-time work but should mean your being available for consultation once a week. Depending on the way it develops, I think this work would entail reading of manuscripts *or* books (almost exclusively English but also some French books), cutting, rewriting and also some pictorial research. Later in the year it may also mean writing of blurbs. For this work you would be paid £70 per month and it would start, if you so wish, on February 1. When you return we shall have to go into the whole question of tax! Your novel will definitely come out in early June or perhaps even late May. The proofs should be with you long before you return.

'I want you to know definitely that if you decide not to return to Cyril you can depend on me to any degree you like. If you can forgive me and curb the grievances and resentments arising out of the post-Westbury phase, please give me another chance. Whatever you may have felt or still feel, believe me, I am just as wretched and perhaps even more wretched than you are, and can only plead weakness and character deficiency. If you have some love left and a little charity you may perhaps give me another last opportunity. But before you leave please let me see you for a little while. I promise you no scenes or hysteria. For one thing, I must explain something about the manuscripts.'

Later, he called to say, 'I have neither the power nor power of persuasion to make you desist from mistrusting me or from deviating from your plan to depart. But I must see you, even if it's only for a little while. I want you back with all the commitments for a saner and happier life. I want to marry you. You could help me to conquer my instability and momentary panics. The nervous crisis and pitched passion I faced manifested itself in a manner both frightening and ignoble. But please remember you have me at your disposal. I want your divorce to go through,' he insisted. 'I do not want to shirk being cited. If you are free you can decide if you want to live with me and marry me or live alone. If you decide the former I shall be there. If the latter, I shall be at your side to help you with all I have. But, please come and spend an evening with me before you leave *without discussion*.'

But I remained adamant.

Chapter V

Morocco

Cyril met me in Tangier. We drove to the Hotel Allard where we found a note from Paul Bowles saying he would be delighted to see us both at seven, and that his chauffeur, Temsamani, would call and pick us up. Temsamani arrived with the painter, Ahmed Yacoubi, and we were driven to a modern apartment block in the residential quarter. Cyril kept saying I resembled 'an oiled gull' and seemed to be completely destroyed.

We continued to see a lot of Paul and his wife, Jane, who lived with Cherifa, a married Arab woman wooed and winkled with difficulty from her husband, in the Casbah, where Daphne and Xan Fielding occupied a house with tortoises crawling about the matting. Jane Bowles was a very witty lady. She had published two original, short masterpieces of wit and style. A novel, *Two Serious Ladies*, written when she was twenty-one years old, had been described by Tennessee Williams as a classic. A collection of short stories, *Plain Pleasures*, was also well received. Then, to everyone's regret she published nothing further; this may have been due to her drinking. It was not for lack of trying, as I remember her saying she intended to incarcerate herself alone in the Casbah in order to get on with some project she then had in mind. Ali Forbes was also in Tangier living in requited love with a very beautiful Moorish girl. When Cyril returned to the Davises in Spain, I spent some nights with her in their flat, Ali having gone off to Cairo to see Nasser. Before going to bed she would carefully place the customary bowl of fresh milk on each window ledge to ward off any lurking evil spirits.

I was very attracted to Paul Bowles. He had natural elegance and charm, spare, perfect features and beautiful tarantula fingers. He grew his own pot, always very fresh and potent, so that I would leave his apartment reeling, having lost all sense of time or purpose. I admired his writing, particularly *The*

Sheltering Sky, and as his conversation was very brilliant, when alone with him I barely uttered. Even so, later on, when he came to London, we met again and on one of his visits to the United States he came to my New York apartment.

Diary

Hôtel Villa de France: Winter in Morocco
Wake up feeling sticky and sluggish. Look out of the window. The whole of the town enveloped in grey; it's drizzling. Reach out of bed and pick up a receiver to ask, 'What time is it?' and order a *café complet*. Continue looking out of the window at a palm, a minaret and beyond the minaret, the blue, white and chrome-yellow rooftops. Think about nothing except what I shall do that day. Without deciding, I continue to lie there and become more despairing.

Then the telephone rings and a voice says, 'How are you? What are your plans today?'

'I don't know exactly.'

'Well, I'm glad you're alright,' says the solicitous voice of Peter Mayne, author of an amusing autobiography, *The Alleys of Marrakesh*. 'I'll telephone again tomorrow and we might meet sometime.' Why not today? I think, but, 'Alright,' I reply. By midday, my gloom having reached a suicidal pitch, I force myself out of bed, and after carefully buttering one roll and jamming the other, I wrap them in a napkin and hide them away in a drawer. An act of thrift in the event of future hunger. In the hall I whine to the girl at the reception about having to pay *demi-pension*.

'Now, it is lunchtime,' I say, 'and behold I'm not at all hungry. This evening I'm asked out. You see, I have many friends here.' After ten minutes' haggle, she agrees to take off fifty *pesetas* each day. Pleased with the transaction, I step out of the porch into torrential rain and decide that, after all, I am ravenous. Go into a smelly Italian café and am given a plate of greasy pork which I eat without pleasure and am handed a bill of 100 *pesetas*.

Go to the post and ask, 'Is there any mail?'

'Nothing,' says the man.

Look into Dean's Bar, it is empty. Dean is seated in a corner reading Rupert Brooke. Make my way in the rain, a scarf over my head, to the Hotel Allard.

'Any mail?' I say. The man hands me a telegram from Cyril which reads: Marbella full but he could get me a room in the Santa Clara for a week.

When the sympathetic lady who runs the Allard hears I'm there, she rings down and says, 'Your husband telephoned yesterday to know how you were. He told me to tell you that he loved you.'

'In that case, why isn't he here?'

'*Les hommes sont comme ça,*' and she smiles.

Hell. I think, since I'm banned from La Consula, I will certainly not go to Torremolinos. And how monstrous it was of Cyril to have left me on Saturday, after I'd taken so many sodium amytals.

'Do you want a doctor?' he had asked angrily, consulting his wrist, momentarily forgetting that he no longer possessed a watch. 'I shall miss the boat. If you want a doctor, say so.'

'I just want to sleep,' I murmured, and turned over as he rushed out slamming the door. I went on sleeping until the following day with occasional visits from the manageress who took up the query of calling a doctor. By Sunday, she was cross.

'You must eat,' she insisted, and handed me an omelette. Very hungry, I ate it and in five minutes fell asleep again.

The following morning, feeling better, I staggered up and packed. It was so cold in the Allard and I had decided to move to a warmer hotel.

'You're not moving somewhere else?' she asked kindly. In order not to offend her, I said.

'To stay with friends. It's lonely here on my own.'

'I understand,' she said.

Yesterday, I lunched with Jamie Caffery and David Herbert, whose Spanish-style house is crammed with parrots, a pug dog, creamy Abyssinian cats, and Victorian and Regency furniture brought over from Wiltshire. David is the Queen of Tangier and how very delightful he is. That evening, I was dining alone in the same restaurant when I overheard a conversation between two English people. One, a rather distinguished old lady, said, 'Did you see David Herbert come in this morning?' Her companion, a priggish young man with a small ginger moustache, nodded. In a horrified tone, the old lady said, 'Did you notice the way he was dressed? An *open-necked* shirt and *no* tie.' She shook her head and added, sadly, 'To think of all the charming people he used to know in Wiltshire.'

Agadir

The wind has abated but the sky is grey with scant patches of blue. The beach curves round to a point and the sands run up into a wood of eucalyptus trees, while the sea creeps gently to shore in smooth, overlapping rollers. Landing at the airport was a great disappointment. It was cold and windy, all the passengers from the plane dispersed and I was the only one to board a bus. The driver said the Mahraba was closed and dropped me off at the Saada, a large honeycomb building, mostly empty.* The wind howled all night and morning. Sent a telegram to Cyril, but the depression saps one's energy, nothing seems worth doing, one's body becomes a load. I tried to read Paul Bowles' new book, *The Spider's House*.

Have a small supply of *kif* in my basket that Paul's American friend gave me, not to be taken all at once, he warned, or I might 'blow my top'. I am not sure I like its effect as much as I used to; it accentuates the mood one is in, therefore, in a state of gloom one becomes suicidal, the fantasies are frightening, one becomes uninhibited and one's mind follows a free-association pattern. The most impossible facts become a conviction.

Giant locusts fly past the window. I leave a message for Mr Corcus to ring me. While in Tangier someone had given me an introduction and described him as being an Anglicised Jew, whereupon David Herbert had clasped my hand and said, 'You like them, don't you, dear?'

I sit in my hotel room and mope a great deal, going over W.'s cables and official letter written from Weidenfeld and Nicolson. The first cable sent care of Paul Bowles' postal box number said I was to reconsider his pleas, that he missed me and that I was to rely on him and return to Chester Square and would I cable a reply, which I did:

> Your words become meaningless since everyone told you want freedom. Your pleas unconvincing, if not why encourage my going? Disheartened by messiness. Allegations proved. Could one consider you reliable? Flying south tomorrow. Love.

His next cable conveyed that there would be no recurrence of events, the idea of him wanting freedom was quite farcical and that separations only bred suspicion, ambiguity and propaganda. Would I please telegraph a few nice words? I was not to prepare for a long stay in Morocco and if I liked he would meet me half-way somewhere. The gist of the official letter from Weidenfeld and Nicolson was that on my return to England they hoped I would be prepared to help as a reader and editorial associate on a part-time basis, at a rate of £500 pa. I would have to attend one or two meetings a week, but for the rest I would not have to be based permanently in London. This arrangement could start on February 1. They could quite definitely commit themselves to a

---

* A year or two after my visit Agadir suffered an earthquake and the Saada collapsed into a mound of rubble. Robin Maugham happened to be staying in the hotel at the time, but he survived several days trapped beneath a concrete block resting on his bedhead before being rescued, unlike most of the inhabitants of Agadir, now rebuilt as a magnetic winter and spring suntrap for tourists.

contract until the end of the year and at the end of the year the contract could be continued automatically. I was to take this as binding and was to let the firm know, formally, say within the next month or two, at the latest, if I accepted. With kindest regards.

I wrote:

Dear George, I am feeling much better and have decided that I would like to take the job as reader at £500 a year, starting from March 1. As I don't want to go back to England until the weather is warmer, would you send the first manuscript with specimen reader's report by air to the British Post Office, Tangier? Review books are sent to Malaga and arrive quite regularly, so I don't see why there should be any difficulty. If you agree to this, would you let me know in the proper manner through the firm, with a contract for a year? I have nothing to read, at the moment, so anything will be welcome. Barbara.

Hotel Mamounia
Ramadan. Three in the morning. The hum of people awakening, a blurr of movement and noise. Dogs bark; there is the sound of flutes and of a mob newly risen to action.

On a walk yesterday, I passed a stream alive with small crabs and bullfrogs, their slimy green heads just protruding out of the water. At six in the evening the sky was a pink violet haze. Standing at his stall, a butcher was chopping entrails surrounded by sleek white cats, their necks craned forward, as they expectantly awaited the drips. A large, fat Arab lady in a white kaftan saw my amusement and her eyes mellowed into a smile behind the blue veil. With great pride, a carpet merchant brought out an old newspaper and from it a prized Chleuh* cloak now only fit for dusters. In a covered yard, an Arab was making tea surrounded by distended goatskins filled with water, the wet, matted hair congealed, and propped on top of each hairy flank was a glass of steaming mint tea, awaiting its owner. It rains and rains. No sun. Grey sky. Giant smuts like black hailstones flit down from the hotel chimney. A fat little bird with a grey-flecked head and long tail like a paper cutter sits on the ledge of the terrace.

The *valet de chambre* returns with my shoes.

'*Déjà? C'est vite fait.*'

---

* A Berber tribe from north Morocco.

34

'*Oui.*' He grins. At the door, he says, 'You stay here long time?'
'I don't know. *Ça depend s'il y a du soleil!*'
'*Ah oui.*' He nods, his mouth wide open showing very good white teeth.
'You here alone?' I laugh.
'*Oui.*'
'You not married?'
'*Si.*'
'*Ahhhh.*' He sighs with relief. '*Ça bon.*'
Three things I want to buy here, a Berber bracelet I saw in the souk, a
handmade blanket and a Berber necklace in the Hotel *vitrine*.

Am debating whether or not to move to a cheaper hotel in the Medina. There
is one called the Central, mosaic floors, a courtyard with a banana tree and a
bougainvillea climbing the cedar wood balustrade. Even there it's not cheap.
Five hundred francs a day. I am in the throes of deciding when the *valet de
chambre* brings me some marigolds.
'From me,' he says.
Feel far less depressed here than in Agadir, where it really seemed to be a
city of the dead. Mr Corcus, rather a disappointment, but very kind, gave me
lunch every day and took me to visit Taroudant and a Moorish market. It is
still raining. But what a beautiful city. The red ochre, palms and minarets, the
snow-capped Atlas mountains, olives and luxury hotel with its beautiful garden
of orange groves. Birds hop timidly across the terrace to peck at the *brioche*
crumbs. Ravens fly low overhead. Have been picked up by a rather jolly
French businessman resembling a grasshopper who calls me 'His Star of the
South' and happily takes me round sightseeing with a guide. He has heart
trouble and has to be in bed by nine.

Peter Mayne's Chinaman, Doan, is a beautiful *tapette*. Attractive and sympathetic with an appreciative sense of humour. We sit in a café on the *place*,
where I try to eat a disgusting bean soup, the mint tea equally disgusting.
Doan says he is writing a book on Indo-China. We talk about dreams. He
always dreams in colour. Have I read Baudelaire on hashish? We agree that *kif*
does not alter one's mood. Despair becomes accentuated. The present more
intense. The fantasies unendurable. In my present state, the paranoia it
engenders is too unpleasant. I shall wait until I'm happy again.
Doan has an eighteenth-century house with stone floors, raffia mats and
heavy cedarwood shutters. It is full of pretty things, a gilded Chinese birdcage

shaped like a pagoda, full of budgerigars, a moorish chest lined with green leather which he has turned into a desk by letting down the flap and illuminating the interior. His friends are waiting in the Café de l'Etoile. They all have the same haircut, clipped close to the head and brushed forward across the brow. One, a doctor, says, in a high-pitched, gentle voice, that yesterday he prepared tea and where was I? How brown I am. He has a catlike tread and a lisp. When asked if he is coming with us to the Arab house for mint tea, he says, 'J'ai un rendezvous.' Then, three of us take a calèche; the French professor and an Arab follow on bicycles.

'Vous êtes la Reine.' Doan laughs, raising his shoulders and laughing as he lingers on the word, Reine. Clop. Clop. Clop.

The middle-aged, goaty one says, 'Comme c'est joli, the sound of the sabots.' It reminds him of some French film. When we draw near to the Porte de Jeudi, the oldest sector of the town, so called as it is next to the Jeudi camel market, one sees an occasional fruitstall lit by one low bulb. Noticing the glow of pipes, I say, 'Regardez! Comme tout le monde fume.' Doan laughs again.

'Eh oui! Et mange et fait l'amour,' lingering on the word amour. He points out each Marabout as we pass.

We have a long wait at the entrance to the Arab house.

'It's always like this,' Doan says. 'There has to be a lot of preparation. And the women got out of the way.'

The room is very clean. The goaty one begins to take off his shoes, but Doan says it's only necessary when there are rugs. There is a low double bed and the usual cushioned bench running along the wall. The boy tells us he has been twice married, the first time at the age of fourteen. He seduced the girl and his father made him marry her. If a wife is unfaithful she goes to prison. When she comes out she can be taken back or can marry again if anyone will have her. The boy asks if I am married and if so why aren't I with my husband?

'Our women are very independent,' Doan says and, turning to me, asks, 'Is that the right reply?'

'You can say I am in a prison like a divorced wife. The Mamounia prison.'

Doan accompanies me back to the hotel. Passing the Turkish baths there are chinks of light in the walls. The Chleuh dancers are still on the place.

'It used to be much livelier before the restrictions,' Doan says. On entering the Mamounia I exclaim,

'Back to my prison.' Doan laughs.

'A prison doré, at any rate.'

On reaching my floor, I hear a woman in the room next to mine screaming, 'You homosexual filth! You homoschizophrenic filth! First Johnny, then Georgy, now Bunny. You're a homo. You're sexual filth who ain't goin' give money to no one. You falling asleep homoschizophrenic filth and I know you from way back . . .' Then a scuffle.

'. . . keep your hands off me . . .' he pleads.

'I'd like to knock your teeth in, you homo, you . . .'

I stand outside my door in my kneelength, corduroy pants listening, when an old lady comes along the corridor. Embarrassed to be seen eavesdropping I am about to return to my room when she stops and whispers in French, 'It's like that every Saturday night. I don't understand what they say, but it's the same every Saturday night.'

'She calls him a homosexual,' I explain.

'*Quel malheur! Quelle tristesse!*' she repeats softly, and passes along the corridor.

Sunday

After a fearful awakening the day got better. But I must not boast too soon. Was given a present of a Moroccan bag by the Frenchman. Then he took me to the Villa Taylor of Churchill fame. We then walked round the souk pursued by a guide who tried to get me to buy in each of the stalls.

Monday

Feel much better and less desperate. Put it down to yesterday's two-hour walk, let's hope it lasts.

The *valet de chambre* just came in bringing my black patent belt that he's repaired. When I offered him 200 francs, he refused and still hung about, so I said, as he had requested earlier, 'Would you like me to take your photograph?' I opened the shutters and put him on the balcony.

'But together,' he said.

'Not with this camera,' I pretended. He grinned and I snapped him like that, grinning like a March Hare.

Cyril rang at seven. He was taking Ali Forbes' Moroccan girl out to dinner.

Tangier

I am here with a party seeing Jane Bowles off to America and have just written to George:

I think it very inconsiderate of you not to answer my letter. It was you who suggested the job as reader and it now looks as though you're going to let me down again. How can I possibly believe what you say in your cables, when you back out of everything?

BARBARA CONNOLLY CARE OF PAUL BOWLES STOP GREATLY DISTRESSED TELEGRAM MARRAKESH RETURNED SINCE YOU LEFT NO FORWARDING ADDRESS STOP PLEASE RETURN AND BELIEVE THAT MY PLEAS ARE SINCERE AND NOT MADE LIGHTLY PLEASE WRITE IT IS VERY URGENT AND I AM VERY UNHAPPY

Me:

> PLEASE TELEPHONE HOTEL VILLA DE FRANCE LATEST TUESDAY,
> BARBARA.

Then:

> TERRIBLY FRUSTRATED TANGIERS LINE OUT OF ORDER TRIED
> REPEATEDLY HOPE BY TIME YOU GET THIS WILL HAVE GOT
> THROUGH IF NOT CABLING LOVE AND AFFECTION.

When he eventually got through on the telephone, he said we had to meet
and that he was flying out to Gibraltar to see me in about a week. Would I be
there? He added that there was a lot of irritating propaganda around which we
must both discount.

I cabled from Gibraltar:

> Don't know where I shall go from here. But it won't be far. Have little faith
> in your coming as you suggested. But if you send a telegram to the Rock
> Hotel, I will leave a message to say where I am and can meet any plane at
> twelve hours' notice.

Chapter VI

Renewals

Diary

Wonderful hot day. Blue sky and calm. See W. off at the airport. Joan Jenkinson, the heiress,* was leaving on the same plane ('Your future wife,' I say jokingly, thinking of her millions). 'That man' very affectionate. Waves back at me as he crosses the runway carrying a despatch case, the GP bag, as I call it. 'You mean like an abortionist?' he says. He stops every few yards to wave back until boarding the plane. I wave back. Once he has gone I realise I am rather relieved; it has been an ordeal of guilt. Last night, I had a terrible guilt dream that I was covered in large, flat-topped bugs like *morpions*, which dug deep into my flesh and could only be removed with a ruler. I awoke with a scream. W. quoted someone as saying that with me he had met his Mrs Simpson and his father had asked him what his relationship with me was. Was it based on sex? W. was going through a grave crisis with Marks and Sparks who were threatening to terminate a book contract he had obtained through his ex-wife, Jane Sieff. He recounted all the gossip. Poppet had said that once, when she was very much in love with someone, I would telephone *every* morning and say, 'Found any faults yet?' Sonia thought I was a heartless liar and nymphoprig, as Cyril calls J., also made some digs. W. said the day his divorce was announced in the newspapers, some people had telephoned to commiserate. One person said, 'Don't feel obliged to do anything, she's over age, after all.' But the fact that he flies out to Gibraltar to see me (like a Governor, as Cyril put it, visiting one of his unruly tribes in order to redress any grievances) denotes some degree of feeling, I suppose!

---

* Lady Sherborne, daughter of the Canadian millionaire, Sir James Dunn.

◇◇◇

March 6 1956

An enjoyable journey on the boat to Algeciras, the half-hour crossing being just sufficient to repack the basket and Moroccan bag, and bask a bit without becoming bored. Bright sun and calm sea. Delighted with the day and the prospect of what I imagine will be a happy marital week with hubby. He grins when I see him approaching on the *quai*, looking suntanned and sweet, his review book under one arm, wearing his food-spattered, brown suede jacket that reeks of bad Tangier cleaning, and I grin back. I am relieved to note that he seems to be in a good humour, without bitterness and pleased to see me. How can I possibly leave him? What is one to do? A long wait on the boat as everyone stands assembled before we are allowed off. Joining him, I say, 'What an intolerable country.' Why were we held up for so long? His good humour diminishes and on entering the customs he is at once in a belligerent mood, refuses to carry any of my luggage, and stands about looking proud and puffy. Was it because I had not shown enough affection?

'Did you go to bed with him?' he asks.

'I am not answering any questions.'

'Then you did. Don't you have any conscience about who would be the father of your child, if you had one? Now that I know you have no moral scruples of any kind, I really must divorce you.'

'But you have started divorcing me already.'

'That is just lies.'

'But it has been in the newspapers.'

'Have you seen them?' says Cyril, as though he had gained a point.

When we reach the hotel, we go into luncheon. Cyril sits snarling and red in the face. Looking down at my wrist and seeing a new bracelet, he says, 'What a dreadful old woman you're going to be, covered in bangles and lonely.' Then he shows me a letter from his lawyer, advising him to carry on with the divorce, and a telegram from the Davises, telling him to join them in England, where they will find him a much better 'pussy'.

'You know what Mr Bulchand, the jewel merchant, said to me on the telephone after seeing you and W.? "That is no man, Mr Connolly. Don't you realise he's just another Sonia with a cock?" Did he ask you to marry him? I'm tired of being the Comic Cuckold. You make me too unhappy.'

'It makes me unhappy knowing that I do. You must go on divorcing me,' I urge.

The lunch is not a success and in the middle of some abusive statement about Poppet, whom I produce as a friend (Cyril having stated I have none), I get up and leave the table, and go and sit in the garden. Presently Cyril comes

40

out and says, Could he have a few words in a more secluded place, as he is leaving? I give in. The abuse starts all over again; he then gets up and disappears.

'Telephone me tonight at the Victoria, Ronda.'

Left alone I feel desperate. What to do? Ring BEA Gibraltar. They say there is a passage tomorrow. I book it and send W. a wire. Feeling deserted I go to the hotel hairdresser. At seven I receive a message written in Cyril's hand, given to someone at the station. If it had come earlier it would have saved the situation. Have a meal in my room. A ghastly night! Woken all night by dogs, a stampede of footsteps along the passage, taps running, cars accelerating, voices, people moving about in the next room, as if we were divided by a thin partition. Feel a wreck. Thinking I am about to leave for Gibraltar, Cyril telephones at seven. State I am incapable of moving. Too tired, look ghastly too, as I have not slept well over the weekend. Cyril suggests we meet at Marbella. I consent. Fall asleep. Wake at nine and telephone BEA, cancelling flight and booking one a week later. Send W. another wire: 'FALSE ALARM STOP RETURNING TODAY WEEK STOP WRITING LOVE.' Order breakfast. Later ring Cyril as the weather has changed, cloudy now, and suggest that we go to Granada instead. Tells me to catch the 3.30 train, passing through Ronda. My bill is enormous – the lunch with Cyril on it and some drinks we had during the bicker. Give the remains of the pesetas that W. gave me, but am adamant about cashing the pounds. Supposing I am left on my own again? The hotel very nice about it, say it is all right and no need to leave luggage. Have a delicious lunch in the hotel of sea bass, described on the menu as sea wolf, steamed and served with melted butter, boiled potatoes and lemon. The young manager comes up and has a friendly conversation about my sheepskin coat, says he has one like it, but has difficulty in getting it cleaned, even in Paris. In Madrid, he tells me, there is a place. Delighted to leave Algeciras. The journey to Ronda of great beauty, valleys, mountains, orange groves, *toros* grazing, white villages, gipsy encampments. Cyril distant and angry-looking, meets me in Ronda with a bag of fried veal in breadcrumbs, tasting of rancid oil, garlic sausage and cheese. Having felt hungry up to then, immediate loss of appetite. Oranges dry and tasteless, too late in the season. At Granada we luckily get a room in a *parador*. We do a lot of sightseeing, me complaining of the amount of walking; get irritated when he loses his way, a certain amount of bickering. The pending divorce a presumed fact.

Am reading a biography of Victor Hugo: 'The great advantage in calling oneself vicious is that it permits one to be vicious' – Sainte Beuve. (Think of W. who is always saying how badly he treats me.)

Cyril and I are now staying at the Hotel Sexi, Almuñecar. It is a cloudy day; the fishermen are laying out their black nets across the sands, white gulls fly above the water, and there is the sound of breakers beating against the rocks and the occasional shout of a fisherman. We have ordered breakfast; the sky is grimly overcast but it looks as though later the sun may break through; behind the spread-out nets is a small shack with 'Bar' written across; a donkey stands mutely by, loaded with packs and large black pigs snuffle about the sand; the sea is outlined by high cliffs, covered in scrub, which curve round to a point. It is so beautiful here, with its custard-apple plantations, loquat, bananas and sugarcanes that stretch out behind the town in long yellow strips bordered by the Sierra de Almijara mountains. We have been taken round all the *fincas* for sale in the vicinity by a boy. When we first picked him up I said to Cyril, 'Ask what he does for a living, what his profession is.'

'There's no need to ask, it's quite clear, his profession is *boy*,' Cyril replied, and made up the following ditty.

> 'There once was an eminent thinka,
> who set his great mind on a *finca*.
> When he bunged in a cheque
> to the owner on spec
> his bank bunged it back with a stinka.'

Last night the *boy* took us to a café to meet his fellow spivs whom he said would sing flamenco, but it turned out to be an equivalent to 'The Witch's Sabbath' — a scene from Goya.

Left Almuñecar yesterday. It was wet and windy. Another bus ride through sugarcane country. After being cut the sugar gets piled into donkey packs and transported to the factories set up in every town, spotted from a distance by the height of the chimneys. Apropos of feeling not at all secure with me now, Cyril said he felt like a dog on a leash; each time he took a leap in the air he was wrenched back by the neck.

Because of the enormous bill at the Hotel Sexi, when we arrived at the Malaga bus terminal, he refused to take a taxi and insisted on walking down the main street carrying my typewriter, basket and Moroccan bag. We then argued about where to stay. I was in favour of pressing on to Torremolinos, as country surroundings are less depressing in bad weather. Cyril grumbly as there has been a muddle over his review book, on Bill's instructions, one copy having been returned to England, another not having arrived. We discussed whether to contact the Bakewells, have dinner or go straight to bed. The noise of hammering and voices induced us to do a tour of the bars. The Mañana was so crowded we bolted to Tommy's and found it deserted. Tommy said business had been bad ever since the opening of the new bar next door.

Doing a trip with the Bakewells in Tommy's white Jaguar. I have had a temperature brought on by sun or from putting off W., as I was due back three days ago. Several times in the night, Cyril said, 'What am I going to do when you go back to England?'

'I don't know, Cyril. It depends on you. After all, the divorce is still going on.'

Well, the affair is now nearing its end. We hope! The final veer on the part of W.

I got back from abroad to find the gaudy, paisley wallpaper lining the stairs had been hung upside down, that he had filled his house with ugly furniture, a set of twelve, highly polished fake Victorian dining chairs and a lot of Peter Jones occasional tables. Then there was a terrible dinner party. The two guests of honour (American publishers) were not exactly sober, dinner was cooked by the Italian servants of tasteless noodle soup and dry veal stuffed with hard-boiled eggs. The wine was vinegary and afterwards came the inevitable chant, 'What are we going to do now?'

And, from then on, he sat about rubbing his brow with an anguished expression on his face, the lips sucked inward to a receding point and the nose a distinguished beak. No doubt he had something to frown about. When he remained in bed I tried to be attentive by taking up delicious things to eat, which he snatched from my hand without showing any appreciation, all the time saying, 'Where's this?' or 'Where's that?' with his mouth full even before I'd had time to eat.

I don't feel upset any more. Each scene has been enacted once too often. First, he insisted on a resumption, without any thought for Cyril's feelings, in order to bide time while his own divorce went through. Then the panic flight from Madrid. My divorce was about to be heard in court and apparently, if it came out in the papers, it would be so bad for business. Added to which, as a result of the cut in the Marks and Sparks contract, he would be so impoverished he couldn't afford me. The telephone was going all the time or he would ring someone to report on his latest business development. Then there were the people who called to invite him to something.

'Oh. May I come? Thank you so much,' he would say with expressionless, unsmiling eyes, 'so much looking forward to meeting you. I would *most awfully* like to . . . thank you so much.'

He seemed to get very upset on discovering it was too late to go to a party. In the morning, Lizzy Lezard had to be telephoned:

'Who was there? What did so-and-so say?' – W.'s expressions in times of stress. 'What's your game?' When I couldn't make an appointment, 'Its not good enough!' When I annoyed him by refusing to do something, 'Come off it!'

When, after a year's wavering, he decided that he had really made up his mind to marry and telephoned to arrange a meeting, I refused, being sceptical and discontented, but he kept saying, 'But this is *it*' – meaning D-Day had arrived. That was a month ago.

I am once more reunited with my husband (without regret) on what he likes to term a 'trial'. 'Poohy' from the bath, as usual, and a lot of 'Poor Baby' mutterings, as well as 'Barbara' in soft, resigned tones. I don't feel too unhappy. Of course, there have been terrible rows, mostly about money. The first night we screamed at each other until we both almost spat blood and there was a lot of, 'Well, why don't you go back to him . . . ?'

'Yes, I probably will.'

We had the genet in the kitchen. What a dull, vicious little animal it is – just spits and stinks and sleeps and shits. I am not yet too unhappy about W. (touch wood). I really do feel myself to be out of the trees – the final change of heart has deadened some original spring of emotion. W. said he was as disappointed in me as I was in him, I forget why; probably because I was not seeing people all the time or talking incessantly on the telephone. What he really wanted, he said, was to come back from the office and find me conducting a cocktail party in the sitting room. There was hardly any pleasure in his company except for the instinctive, animal desire to be near one's mate. We never had a mutual thought or opinion and didn't even like the same people.

On receipt of my letter asking to have some clothes returned, he telephoned yesterday and said, 'Can we meet sometime soon or can I telephone more often?' How could two people who had been so close break away so finally and abruptly? When I said, 'No,' there was a choking sob the other end.

I go over the past, relishing every detail as one might mull over a good dinner without wishing to eat it again unless desperately hungry. But the full heat of the fever is past and how did it come about? Was it because of his character defects, as C. prophesied? Since the divorce is still going through, C.

says he wouldn't mind so much my seeing W. in London, but he gets into a tizzy when he telephones and shrieks, 'I would like to kill that man.'

Another really hot day. Almost unbearable. As usually happens in England, when it does arrive, intolerable. Cannot put my mind to anything. Feel bewildered, sapped of all zest. Do not know what I feel about the two heroes, the *maquereau* and the *salaud*, so called, from my vague description of them both, by the Frenchman I met in Marrakesh.

Am seeing W. again. This time, all Feliks' fault. When I told him that although I had returned to Cyril, he was still going on with the divorce, first giving as a reason to start afresh in a church, the next minute saying artists are not meant to marry, Feliks then said, 'Well, I wouldn't have mentioned anything if things had been going well with you, but W. has been on to me night and day, and now says that as soon as the divorce is through he will meet you at Caxton Hall.' So I weakly telephoned and have been having secret meetings ever since, but when he talks of marriage, I cannot take it seriously; in fact, would not really want it. I find living with him lonely and barren . . . the telephone calls, rushing out to have pointless drinks, the unsympathetic house. But I can barely enter Chester Square, I am so terrified of being seen, and yet I do not have the courage to tell W. that I do not want to marry now.

Have just come from London. Spent the evening with W., his last before flying to Israel. He was never off the telephone. A lot of *turnover* talk. Cyril had dinner with the Flemings who abused me in venomous terms.

'What did you have to eat?' I asked, knowing the usual form.

'Unripe avocados and some rather dull little soles.'

W. is back from Israel. He seems very concerned about his weight. Never stops staring at himself naked in the mirror, half in wonder, half in doubt.

'I'm thinner, don't you think?'

Have now been divorced three weeks. C. let the absolute go through in the same way as the hearing in court, telling me *afterwards*, clearly terrified that I was going to take some action to thwart it. I got panic-stricken the morning of the absolute, just felt something terrible was taking place, so I consulted a lawyer who listened to everything I had to say and then advised against getting on to the Queen's Proctor. Said the husband would always bear resentment and would a remarriage work out? I said, 'I shall be a pauper and starve to death.'

'From the sound of it,' the lawyer said, 'your husband will always provide. What about the Co-Respondent? Won't he support you?'

'I think it goes against the grain for either of them to support a wife,' I said jokingly. The lawyer looked startled, but offered no contradiction.

C. then rang and said the object in going through with the divorce had been to 'see' W. (as in poker) with me as the stake.

'And if I actually do marry him,' I said, 'how will you feel?'

'Like someone who has missed a close putt on the last green of a championship.'

When I rang W. at his office to give him news of the absolute, he metaphorically put his head in his hands and, after a long pause, groaned, 'Now, what are we going to do?'

The following day I got a letter from C., written on Ritz Hotel notepaper.

Darling Love,

For the first time I feel that I have done something cruel to you and for which I can ask you to forgive me, like the cruel things you have done to me in the last year — it purges me of all resentment and it makes me only want to deserve your love. If you had been anywhere but in Chester Square I would never have done it. I enclose six cheques for twenty pounds each, payable monthly, which I regard as your housekeeping allowance. If you are still on your own, they will go on, but if you marry Weidenfeld, they will stop. The moment I am with you again they really become your housekeeping money and I will give you a further twenty a month for your clothes. The rest of my salary we will supervise together. This twenty is only a minimum on the assumption you are also receiving an allowance from Weidenfeld. If this is not the case, please let me know. I still don't think you should take his job, unless you are going to marry him. It is a painful dependency and will cause talk, and affect you adversely. If you can wait until your book comes out, you will be amply rewarded . . .

Have now taken a room on my own in Chesham Place and ceased all sexual relations.

Slim, elegant Mrs Barbara Connolly spent the Bank Holiday with her ex-husband at her cottage near Elmstead, Kent. Mr Cyril Connolly – Britain's portentous literary critic and man of letters -- divorced her four months ago. Are they planning to remarry?

'Not for the moment,' said Mr Connolly. 'Ask me again in a month's time. I may have news for you.' When asked if he hoped that everything would come out right in the wash, Mr Connolly said, 'Yes.'

Well, the book is out, not nearly as bad as one thought it would be. Clearly I am an unconscious exhibitionist. I welcomed all publicity. Ian Fleming gave it a mention in the 'Atticus' column, headed '*Du côté de chez Connolly*'.

In 1950 she married Cyril Connolly and has since lived in Kent where her open Sunbeam Talbot, flashing through the meadow-sweet round a blind corner, is a familiar hazard. She has an Abyssinian cat, is an expert cook (Provençal style) and her slim figure can often be glimpsed, lonely and elegant, meditating during the luncheon hour in some London gallery.

◇◇◇

Never thought I would dare to face the reviews without having them vetted first, but not a bit of it. I grab hold of every newspaper and become riveted to each page as though held by a magnet. Luckily, they have been rather good. Tony Powell wrote and complimented me, and Angus Wilson wrote to say he had found it very funny and tremendously realistic of all the horrors of wartime jobs. Quite a relief after running into the Quennells on the train (who were po-faced) and receiving an anonymous letter from Bexhill:

Dear Madam,

I was attracted by the dust cover of your first and I hope *only* book, *A Young Girl's Touch*. You were lucky to get anyone to publish it; one of the firm is presumably a German – Weidenfeld – it is a horrible and sexual book, and should be withdrawn from all public libraries. What a heroine! I hope she is not drawn from anyone in the Services. Please never write another book.

Disgusted . . .

47

Chapter VII

De la Folie Totale

The marriage to W. took place in late summer, the year of the Hungarian rebellion and the Suez crisis, at Caxton Hall, with our witness, Anne Bassett. I was joined in matrimony with Cyril's emerald engagement ring, an item the future husband had overlooked. A feeling of utter despair followed the ceremony. Then, the newly weds and witness partook of a ritual lunch at the Savoy. A wedding party was given by the millionaire, Charles Clore. When he heard of the marriage, the editor of *L'Oeil* Georges Bernier, is reported to have said, *'C'est de la folie totale.'*

The honeymoon was spent on the island of Ischia. Cyril participated in his fashion from the far end of the island, where he was staying with Wystan Auden.

When not taking radioactive mud baths, I swam on some slatey beach while W., barefooted, with rolled-up city trousers, lay close by, buried in newspapers.

The presumption was that the marriage could not possibly last. Would I release him in an amicable manner after three years?

Marriage was for material betterment, social advancement or to proliferate. Would we part friends? To tease him, I said I could never face another divorce and, leaning forward, stressing each world, I chanted, *'Until death do us part.'* At once the distressed bird-face appeared, eyes bulging while he chewed at his lower lip.

Evening conversation: 'Is it true that so-and-so had an affair with Cecil?' 'Is it true that Tom Driberg wanted to marry Joan?* 'Really, you are like a stone to talk to.' 'But you only like talking gossip.'

---

* In his posthumous autobiography, *Ruling Passions*, Driberg made it clear that one such passion, his homosexuality, coupled with his inability to have a sexual relationship with anyone in his own milieu, had condemned him to a life of utter loneliness.

I began to have nightmares, in one of which I was being followed about by a large male torso with a doorknob for a head.

From then on, when not staying with the Davises, or in Brussels with Hansi Lambert (née Rothschild), a literary and musical lady of the Belgian banking family, C. took a room in Chesham Place. The lemur Wirra landed up with Gavin Maxwell, author of *A Ring of Bright Water*, and I moved into Chester Square with Didessa, the Abyssinian cat, and the genet. This pretty feline, the original cat of ancient Egypt, described as a miniature dinosaur wearing a leopard-skin coat, had spent so much time being caged that it remained adamantly untamable, and skulked under the floorboards and, when it emerged, got swept round the house by the Italian servants, Enzo and his wife, whose culinary speciality was a kind of toad-in-the-hole, a dish that caused me great embarrassment when handed round to dinner guests – the Kilmartins or Graham Greene, who tactfully came to dinner clasping my book for signature, saying, 'Whatever do you, don't remain a one-book woman.'

As I sat sulkily at the head of the master's table, W. would approach the buffet and whisper over my shoulder, 'Gush! Gush! You simply must be more gushing.'

Guests like the Rt. Hon. Lord Hore-Belisha, though, maintained they had had a good and pleasant dinner with interesting talk, the Lord adding that he thought the house a *palazzo*!

W. approved of my lunching with the authoress, Jane Howard.

'That's good. We would like to have her as a reader one day.' He was also pleased when I went to see Tilly Losch.

C. then became the insistent telephoner and sometimes, when I went out to shop, I would find him awaiting me in a taxi in the square. If I appeared reluctant to meet, he accused me of being utterly callous. Wasn't it my fault that he no longer had a home or a wife? He would look at me with baleful, hunted, animalish eyes, while his nose wrinkled with contempt as he spoke of the three untalented females, Janetta, Sonia and Joan, as the professional mourners at a funeral, riddled with envy and revelling in disaster. He seemed so unhappy and this increased my feelings of guilt, and in an effort to cheer him up, I would take little home-cooked dishes round to his room in Chester Place.

Three months after the marriage W. left for New York. The first cable informed me that he and Feliks Topolski had arrived safely. On his arrival there had been millions of messages. He had lunched with his agents. Afterwards, regular bulletins arrived from the Hotel Gladstone giving details of what he had been doing.

'Just digested a yoghurt and cream cheese sandwich.' 'Just read the *Herald Tribune*.' 'Am about to drag myself exhausted into bed.'

I was kept informed of everyone he was seeing: Phillip Rahv of *The Partisan Review*, Charles Rolo and Cass Canfield of *Harper's Bazaar*, Jean Campbell, Beaverbrook's grand-daughter (who later married Norman Mailer), Philippe Jullian and Carmel Snow; of all the luncheons, cocktails, dinners and parties that were being given for him. He had dined with William Faulkner and Jean Stein, had had drinks with Cecil Beaton, been taken to an enjoyable party given by Leo Lerman, editor of *Mademoiselle*, who had invited all the leading actresses and singers, including Maria Callas, then at the Met. He had dined with Israel's envoy to the UN and other Israelis. The Sylvester Gates were there. The Milsteins were taking him to the opera. Tilly Losch was taking him and an ancient New England banker to an O'Neill play. He had made good friends with a Californian senator, oilman and ex-deputy Secretary of State who had invited us both *firmly* to stay at Pasadena during the summer or autumn. (And how!) Feliks was having a *succès fou*. During Thanksgiving, W. hoped to be able to relax from the terrifying routine, stay in and read a vast number of manuscripts. I was the loveliest of wives. He was already missing me, but he was sure I would have hated the life of telephoning and restless rushing around. Everyone knew the full story of our courtship and considered the 'saga' to be very romantic. He hoped to be able to borrow some money to buy me some clothes, including a skirt and top for evening wear. It was too early to say how successful the trip had been. But, already he was on to the track of two or three good books, with unrequited love . . .

By then, I suppose, I had become peevish at being excluded from this whirl of activity and he wrote complaining of my silence. He had written four letters and I only one. I was wrong to attribute volatility and superficiality to be his most outstanding attributes. He considered he had had a wonderfully successful business tour, far above his expenditure, but it would make the firm considerably stronger and sounder. What news of home, the pusscat and why did I gloss over all my activities? He was due back in a week. Would I write giving some news? I was not to make him feel fretful and unhappy. He arrived back on Pan-Am on December 11.

A lot of blame shifting. He had never wanted to marry me. I am responsible for everything going wrong. Rings up from office at twelve o'clock to say he is bringing someone back for luncheon.

I say, 'There is only an omelette and some cheese. Is it enough?'

'Oh yes, a very light luncheon will do.'

But in the middle of lunch he rushes up to me and complains about having to send Enzo out for some meat. Wishes to find fault as much as possible in order to build up a good case against me. Has described it to Sonia as a modern marriage – i.e. experimental. Compares himself to Napoleon and me to Josephine, who was paid off and remained a mistress while Napoleon made a second dynastic marriage. Says half of him wants it to last and the other half not. Main topic always: money. His great fear: sinking into a life of middle-class impoverishment. Cyril ran into Olga Davenport at the Tate.

'I heard you had married again!'

'How do you mean, "Again"? Aren't you confusing me with Barbara?'

'Oh, we all know about that,' she sneers.

'How can I marry again,' says C., 'when I'm still married to B.? I'm a Christian, you see.'

I have a terrible cold. Muzzy head. Dazed. Lack of energy, no appetite.

'Must I go on sleeping with the cat on the bed?' says W.

'Where else should she sleep?'

'Everyone is horrified at my having to sleep with a cat.'

'Who is everyone?'

'Lizzy.'

'Well, since I have to put up with Lizzy, why can't you put up with the cat?'

Wakes up saying he had to go to bed so early; he hasn't been able to sleep *all* night. I say, Is it my fault that I don't feel well and went to bed early? He says, Well then, he should have been able to go out and see his father. I say, But surely, this is the time to stay in, if your wife is not well?

On Sunday, he is out to dinner. On Monday, he has a male dinner party. I might as well make a date every evening on my own.

'We have been asked to dinner by Lady Norton,' he says.

'I will not be well enough to go . . .'

'You want to ruin me. Destroy me. Everyone warned me!'

'Why did you break up my marriage then . . . ?'

'Everyone said you were unhappy . . .'

'I was not unhappy . . .'

'Then why didn't you stay with your husband . . . ?'

'Because I was in love with you.'

Enzo comes in to say the cat has made a mess on the chair cover. At this, both master and servant – Leporello – exchange suffering looks. W. blows up and throws my box of kleenex on to the floor. I am made to inspect the mess in the drawing room. Clearly the cat was shut in and could not get out during the night, peed in the grate, clambered over the coal and from there strolled round the room over the chair cover. She is in disgrace.

'You have got us both into trouble,' I say to her.

W. returns from the office around six o'clock. He bursts into the bedroom, sees me lying on the bed and glares. I glare back.

'Must you lie in bed all day? It gives the servants such a bad impression.' He poses his face into a smile, while his eyes remained deadpan. 'What's new?'

'Nothing special.'

'Anyone telephone?'

He collapses on to the chair with his legs outstretched, starts rubbing the fingers of one hand into the palm of the other and smoothing his forehead. This goes on in silence for some time.

'Has so-and-so telephoned? Will I be a success, do you think? I wish I could get Clore to do something; just lending his name would be enough.'

Christmas

Cries of 'Get out! Get out!' to the pusscat. W. playing the radio and doing his accounts. Talk at lunch. Money. Income tax to pay. Having to support his parents in 1959. I say, 'Why look so far ahead? Anything might have happened by then.' He says I give him a feeling of isolation. He cannot talk to me about his business. I say, 'But you always told me you could never talk about anything with Jane . . .'

'She would always talk about *business*,' he says. Says he has telephoned Sonia and Janetta to wish them a Happy Christmas. He then asks me if I wouldn't like to live in Mexico. *It is very cheap living there.* We both decided the marriage cannot possibly improve. We spend the morning in separate bedrooms. I then get up and make a delicious luncheon. A *Boulestin* recipe, chicken *sauté* with capers, some very good buttery mashed potato and excellent salad of lambs' tails. Discuss whether I would go back to Cyril. W. says, 'You may be sure he wouldn't want to remarry. He might like to live with you if you were provided with some money, but would pursue his own life, dining out with other people.' Think of my lunch with Cyril yesterday; told him W. and I had discussed a separation plan by which I left him – and we divorced on desertion! Cyril's role now that of an advisor.

'You could try and make your marriage better by having a child,' he said.

Since he has adopted this giving-advice line of how I could improve the marriage, I said, 'The best way of improving it, actually, is for you to leave the country, as you are the biggest wedge between us so far.'

Now we never sleep in the same bed. I have moved into the passage room across the landing. Very noisy in the early morning. I am sometimes invited into the treble-size couch. Then the telephone rings, and W. says,

'Is the Blow marriage on or off? Is she playing him up, do you think? Okay, all the best, goodbye.'

Then, turning to me: 'I've come to the conclusion you're mad . . .'

'Why?'

'Because you can't admit being in the wrong.'

'But that's not mad.'

'Yes it is, it's psychopathic.'

Spends all his mornings throughout Christmas lying in bed palm-rubbing against a moist forehead, racking his brain for someone to telephone, while I out of boredom noted down the conversation.

'George here. Okay, old boy. God bless you. To cut a long story short . . . a firm turnover of £50,000, it also produces prints for office diaries . . . an enormous future . . . all books are declining . . . well, I asked him the price . . . purchase profit . . . cheaper . . . instalment system . . . solicitors, don't you agree? . . . negotiate valuation of stock . . . we must be ruthless . . . utmost skill in negotiation, I personally think [silence] Ya! Ya! We've got to think . . . negotiate . . . this is the point . . . got those figures . . . maybe Clore . . . shareholders . . . investment between half a million to three quarters . . . expand business side . . . see what I mean? . . . sell . . . raise money . . . slash the brains . . . sales manager . . . promotion . . . excellent.'

Have been in the house all day; exhausted after going to the Milton Shulman party. Found one person I could talk to about Spain, the Brenans, Davises, Almuñecar. Sonia arrives, makes an ostentatious cut, looks sallow, puffy and shiny, wearing an odd shirt, with a full red skirt and squat blocks protruding from her hem, coloured glass costume jewels, dangling chunky earrings; a mop of blonde straggles, gets shinier and more vociferous as the evening goes on. First person I spot on entering is Kenneth Tynan. Think: Ah! Someone I can talk to. He is sitting on a sofa surrounded by people, all conversing together; he remains slightly apart, silent, and stares rather critically round the room. I wend my way towards him; seeing me he immediately becomes engrossed in animated conversation with Eric Ambler and talking for all he is worth. I halt my pace and turn to face three men grouped together *en route* to the sofa. One of them gets me a whisky. I talk about being cooped up over Christmas, say that this is the first time I have been out and I feel like an invalid with sealegs; no one reacts: I say what a state our house is in, the servants having been on strike. They stare back as though I am being uppish and boasting – a spoilt woman's prattle. Am cut short by one of them pointing to a Lowry painting. In the meantime, Tynan has risen, is obliged to pass by me, says 'Hello', and then bolts across the crowded room and is next seen, looking panicky, with his coat over one arm. I look round for Mrs T., but I fail to identify her, as always, in spite of her resembling a Boucher girl, accordingly to Cyril. Good humour dispelled and spirits flag. Am shepherded by the hostess to the buffet.

'I've not been out of the house for three days.'

'I know what that means,' she brightly replies, laughing.

'Nothing but rows.'

'Exactly.'

Everyone gets seated. W. somehow finds himself sitting next to me and becomes sulky. The woman on his left is Austrian.

'Who is that next to you?' she asks.

'My wife.' She looked amazed. 'Why? Don't you like her?' he asks, half-hopefully.

'Very interesting . . . but not malleable. It won't last. I am a gipsy,' she says finally. W. cheers up on hearing this. When we get home, the usual talk: his business, the only solution is to marry an heiress. He says he cannot go on living in an atmosphere of boycott and blames me. I am determined not to see C. but find myself weakening when he telephones. Hopeless.

W. comes back this evening with a croaky voice, says he does not feel at all well. At once collapses on the bed. Many telephone calls with the family. Hear his mother say, 'Have you got the fire in your room?' – a dig at me; I knew that would be one of the complaints, that I am hogging the electric fire. He orders some coffee, sausage and cod's roe on toast.

'You cannot be so bad if you are hungry,' I say.

Mother rings again; father is coming round with a doctor. They come, doctor stays a second, pronounces him okay. Father remains by the bed for two hours. There is complete silence in their room. I wonder what they can be doing. Enzo is summoned several times. I feel a complete outcast, a lodger in this domain. The servants are leaving in a week. The mother is commissioned to find a replacement. I am not even given any housekeeping money. Says he wants to fall in love again.

'If you want to, then you will,' I say. He does not love me to the same extent, has not done so since October. It is a terrible situation.

'What have I got myself into?' he sighs.

'Cut your losses,' I tell him. 'Now, while the going is good and get out as soon as you can.' His face brightens.

'Do you really mean it?' and he is happy for a fraction of time.

Much talk of separation. Talks of my deserting and agrees to settle for £500. I say I will not consider desertion; I cannot live on £500 a year. My mind soggy and blank from not putting it to any use. Just brushed the cat. Cyril talks of going to the Canaries. Long, long empty days. Servant trouble. They are leaving tomorrow.

'And what do you do for me?' W. asks.

'I am quite split in two. If I get out of touch with Cyril, even for a week, I become miserable. C. admits that he didn't envisage this situation, thought that either I would have returned to him by now, or that he would have found someone else, or have become swept into a more amusing social life. The amusing party life, he thinks, revolves round the Tynans. Says he is now tired of seeing his friends. He has considered marrying various people, including Janetta, who is anxious to marry, but just imagine the wedding party, with all the 'old hats' – Mark Culme-Seymour, ex-lovers, Ralph and Frances Partridge and the Campbells. Clearly, what he really needs is someone young and entirely new.

W. in a dismal voice to his father:

'God knows what sort of a year it's going to be.' A long pause and no reply. Five minutes later, 'I start this year with great financial worries.' They both look at me – the cause of it all.

'Mustn't give up hope,' says father, 'do the best you can.'

Completely listless and apathetic. Living on sleeping pills.

'We must have a serious talk this evening,' he says and dashes off to the office.

In the evening bursts into my room, drops his attaché case to the floor and says, 'Who's telephoned today?' His bed very soon strewn with publicity magazines; he flicks rapidly through the pages, then picks up the telephone. 'To cut a long story short . . .'

Next morning he says, 'We must have a serious talk this evening,' and dashes off to the office. In the evening he returns looking most displeased, remains silent and twitchy about the nose, bites his cuticles, picks his nose and farts. I light the coal fire, hang up a picture and try to make the sitting room habitable. Long, strained silences. Occasionally he looks up to say, 'Do you think we are mad?'

'You may be. I know I'm not.'

'What are we going to do? The next time it must be a total separation.'

One hour later, seated before the fire, he groans and mutters, 'Domesticity.'

Half an hour later: 'What a pity we can't have the ideal situation. You, married to an amenable husband in the country, coming to London twice or three times a week.'

In the morning, he says, 'Tonight, we really will discuss things.' Closes his bedroom door softly. Telephones Bedbug.* I pick up the extension. Says the reason he missed her drinks party last night was because he was ill. She sounds a little peeved. He begs to see her some time over the weekend. She cannot. She eventually agrees to see him that evening at seven. I then overhear him arrange to meet a Pole straightaway *en route* to the office.

On his way out, he comes into my room and says, 'Tonight at seven I'm having a drink with Baroness Budberg to meet a Pole.'

'Now why do you lie? I say. 'I know the Pole won't be there.'

He repeats the story of how he should have gone to see her yesterday to see the Pole, but that she has now rearranged the meeting. I repeat, 'Now why do you lie? I know the Pole won't be there.' And so we go on, but he persists, so that although I had actually heard to the contrary – having listened in to the conversation on the extension – I begin to doubt whether in fact I *had* heard right.

No servants. W.'s spirits low. No one ever rings up now. Terrible scenes about money.

'And what about the cigarettes? There are no cigarettes in the house'.

'Lizzy brings his own. All you want is another row. Just because those hideous little boxes aren't filled with stale tobacco . . .'

'Why can't you buy cigarettes? You have no idea how to run a house.'

'All right!' Screams of hate. 'I'll go out and buy some! Now find something else to row about . . .'

Situation at its nastiest. Having failed to build up a case against me for being a drug addict, cruelty (hogging the electric fire) or got me to agree to an amicable separation, he is trying to sue on grounds of infidelity, citing Cyril as Co-Respondent.

---

* Moura Budberg (Maria Ignatievna)

A great check-up going on. My keys have disappeared, including the one to my Regency table where my diaries are kept. Immediately telephone Mummy who takes a taxi to the cottage and removes the table. Long conversations with parents. Father kept on permanent duty his end of the line. Another hysterical scene, curtailed by me and the immediate administration of a tranquilliser, almost by force, thereby stalling a doctor. He is in a constant touch with lawyers.

Now only speaks to use threats.

'You weren't going to have it all your own way!' Has definitely got something on C. Consults lawyer (new one) daily. Yesterday came running into my bedroom and announced dramatically, 'Situation *very tense.*'

'Oh, is it?' I was lying in bed reading.

'Terrible tension,' he repeats, meaning me to question him. 'Ghastly we should be under the same roof.' (He meant while he is trying to prove something on me and Cyril.) 'Once I get the evidence,' he taunts, 'just think, we won't be able to fuck. It will be condoning.'

'Just think,' I say.

'Sinner,' he goes on, 'how you have deceived me!' His manner is arch, but he seems disappointed that I don't respond by looking stark-eyed.

Today, when I left the house, an Austin Seven was parked at the kerb. When he saw me, the driver quickly revved into gear and proceeded to tail me along Chester Square. Whereupon I hurried down a sidestreet; there was a screech of brakes and, turning, I saw the driver frantically trying to reverse, as I disappeared out of sight.

W. has now moved out of the house altogether. His mother has taken over. The fridge is stacked with kosher butter. She sleeps on a campbed in the hall and yesterday burst into the sitting room as though expecting to find me spread-eagled *delicto* on the couch.

Me dazed and collapsed with fatigue. Cannot stop sleeping. I must have been under a greater strain than I realised over the last weeks.

Chapter VIII

Divorce Proceedings

There was no further contact with W., except through lawyers. He did ring up once, though, and sounded very upset. I only had time to say, 'What's the matter, George? Tell me, what's the matter?' before he had hung up. Brien How, an old friend from Blitz days, happened to be lunching with me and rather callously remarked that it was simply a 'put on', as he wanted to get me to comply with his wishes. But I suppose it must have seemed rather tough luck, paying a lawyer to tell you to get out of your own house. I had not seen Brien since he left Hong Kong, where he became the Chief Magistrate in Kowloon and married a Chinese girl. He preferred the Chinese, he said, as they were far more *fidèle* and devoted than European women. This turned out to be our last meeting. Years later, when he had returned to Europe, he tried unsuccessfully to get in touch again but died of cancer soon after, in Spain.

I don't remember pining for W. any more. The intense physical obsession, comparable to some raging, unprecedented fever, had abated. I don't think you can love someone whom you find inestimable. With an *amour fou*, of course, the subject does not have to inspire admiration. I appreciated W.'s drive, resourcefulness and resilience, and being such a worldy, ambitious man, his intense pursuit had had the temporary effect of making me feel an adult member of society as opposed to a worthless drifter.

Citing Cyril could not be described as being a very laudable act. For we had become a reporter's delight and Cyril risked being dismissed from *The Sunday Times*.

Those three names crop up again. Wealthy publisher, Arthur Weidenfeld, is seeking a judicial separation ... and the man he's citing is her ex-husband ... which makes a change from the position two years ago ...

The only evidence W. had to go on was a visit Cyril and I had taken to the cottage when W. was in the States. Cyril needed to go through his possessions and remove some of his books. We were driven down in a hire car. The chauffeur, Nixon, turned out to be a most amiable fellow. His real profession, he claimed, was that of professional ballroom dancer. When he heard us discussing what to do with Cyril's precious silver, Nixon claimed to have access to a safe and we trustingly handed it over.

We went to the country a second time and stayed a few days. No secret was made of the fact. Whenever a telegram arrived from New York, the maid at Chester Square would telephone. My diary conveys that much as I loved Cyril and often though I thought that the break-up had been a mistake, I realised we could not have gone on living in such close proximity because of the drudgery, endless housework, aching back and wrist from constant stoking of the fire. I suppose by then I had become spoilt. Also, there were Cyril's moods.

I felt sorry for him, of course, but he was always gloomy about something. Then, it was the future, thinking of when W. got back. In the confined cottage surroundings, one person's bad mood was so inflicted on the other as to make life sometimes intolerable. Even the mutterings of 'Barbara! Barbara!' while lying on his bed made me cross and he complained about my angry 'despatch rider's face', although we did get on terribly well, and I felt he understood and forgave me more than anyone else would.

I had been back in Chester Square some time when Nixon telephoned to say he was out of a job. The Italians had gone and W. had been in touch with a Mayfair domestic agency. One illiterate applicant wrote from Wales to say, 'I have heard that you require a General Man Servant the Post I am requiring I have been living with Lady "Tartempion" at Princes Gate for a number of years doing the cooking and cleaning with Daily Help. Lady "Tartempion" has passed away a few weeks ago and her daughter that is living in Gloucester who is giving me the references which I am sending you. Should you think me suitable . . .' But we didn't and offered Nixon the job, and he moved into the spare ground-floor room. Nixon looked presentable. He answered the doorbell, made amusing observations through the kitchen hatch as he tugged at a rope for the food trolley to mount to the dining room, where I stood to receive it. Then he waited at table and, at this stage, I often found his company less of a strain than that of a fretful husband. But whereas Nixon had liked Cyril and taken good care of his silver, he took against W. and one fine day he bolted with all W.'s shirts, leaving his room strewn with cigarette stubs and empty bottles of whisky. Daimler Hire hinted that he was no longer in their service, due to a similar offence. They had no forwarding address and that was the end of Nixon.

For the final weeks in Chester Square, I no longer had a pusscat. She had disappeared and I missed her terribly. She used to follow me about everywhere, even when curled asleep; if I got up to leave the room she would awaken and follow me. Pedigree cat-breeders are usually very endearing ladies. I wrote to a Mrs Stewart to tell her how sad I was and asked her to reserve me a kitten from the next litter, one that most resembled Didessa, who had not been without certain flaws in her ticking, like a touch of black under the chin and on the end of her tail. A month later, Mrs Stewart wrote to say that she had just heard from the Cat Club secretary of an Aby found wandering round Chelsea; 'And wouldn't it be wonderful if it turns out to be your Didessa?' I contacted the couple who had picked up the Aby and arranged a meeting. It was Didessa. But when I saw how she was being treated, like the veritable queen that she was, lying contentedly in a cushioned basket surrounded by playthings, and how this elderly, childless couple doted on her, my life being in a turmoil, I did not have the heart to take her back.

With further divorce proceedings underway, Sutro once more came to the fore as my go-between, pursued by Marreco, acting for W., whose publishing associate he then was. They had no conclusive evidence of infidelity and wanted Sutro to persuade me not to fight the case, but give in to an amicable separation. Detectives had been sent down to the cottage to find witnesses. Our last char, Mrs Golding, had refused to talk and sent me a note saying, 'I hope you are well I hope I can still work for you as I like working for you we have known one another so long I will always stand by you and help you in all ways as you know I wouldn't say anything against you. Yours faithfully . . .'

But the old gardener, Coombes, to whom Cyril had paid vast sums, appeared willing to go into court and give detrimental evidence. And somebody referred to as 'the unknown man' claimed to have seen Cyril and me standing stark-naked in the porch one November afternoon, which was, of course, most incriminating.

In the meantime, Sutro had found me a top-floor flat in Belgravia. No 3 Lyall Street had been bought by a company who eventually planned to install a lift and modernise the building. So it was only a temporary lease. The two top floors were quiet and sunny, and if my life had been more settled, I would have been very happy living there.

A restorer of old paintings, Peter Tunnard, occupied the ground-floor flat and just below me Claus Bulow lived with a beautiful blonde who finally left him for the conductor, Karajan. My two top floors had been empty so long that they needed redecorating. I was still under surveillance, continually peering out of windows, convinced I was being watched. Oddly enough, it was W.'s mother who found me a painter, a handsome man in his fifties, who, one afternoon, when I went round to see how the work had progressed, actually grabbed me by the waist in a whirling embrace and invited me out to dinner. Also, about this time, when I took the train to the country, a harelipped man engaged me in conversation and, when we arrived at Ashford, he insisted on accompanying me to the cottage, only to find Mummy sitting happily chainsmoking in the porch. This man went on haunting me and one day admitted he made a habit of sleuthing.

Sutro kept me informed of the latest developments in the case and, should I be in the country, his secretary, who never had anything to do, typed out a report like the following:

December 6 1957

Today Marreco telephoned me, in the first place about a magazine selling English goods in America. He then said he would like to talk to me personally; I said that whilst he could mention anything to me he liked, I was keeping completely out of this matter which was not in the lawyers' hands. Marreco then said that the case had been set down for trial and will, presumably, come on in approximately February 1958. He said that he personally felt that the case, if fought out, would be detrimental to everybody concerned and he did not deny that it would be detrimental to W., who felt that the odds were definitely in his favour and on the advice of Counsel (Fearnley-Whittingstall) felt obliged to go ahead but would still very much prefer to avoid any contested action on which large fees would be paid to lawyers. Marreco, speaking on W.'s behalf, wished that the case should not be defended; that both sides should pay their own costs; and then W. would finally settle the existing dress bills and continue the present payments to you until the date of the decree absolute. I said that as far as I knew this had all been discussed by the lawyers already and was completely unacceptable; that I doubted very much whether I could even speak to you about this matter.

Marreco suggested that I meet W. and have a discussion; I said that I could see no possible reason or justification for this. I also said that I did not think the solicitors on either side, certainly not on your side, would consent to any such arrangement as was now put forward. All question of the unknown man, apparently, has now been dropped and the full-scale offensive is being directed towards the question of costs which, it is suggested, would have to be borne by C., if he does not win the case.

The position which I have maintained throughout was that nothing whatever except desertion could ever be considered and that this could be discussed between the lawyers.

If you were to ask me, 'What should I do?' this is always a terribly hard thing to answer on a matter which so vitally affects your whole life. It would depend entirely on the judge alone, or the judge and jury accepting and understanding the fineness of the points which relate to the physical feelings with regard to W. and C. But undoubtedly whilst from your point of view these are straightforward and not difficult to explain in cross-examination, it will not be so easy for C. He will, however, be a very good witness and will explain the reasons why he saw you and why he went to the cottage to deal with his things. The whole weight of the other side will be based on matters like the days spent in Ischia with C., the meetings afterwards in London, and they will do all they can to blur the vital distinction between affection and friendship, and the physical matter which, after all, was the cause to a considerable degree of the break-up of your marriage to C. The only way, presumably, in which the visit to the cottage can be satisfactorily explained is to say that it was not kept a particular secret.

Having convinced himself of the righteousness of his case, W. will in every way endeavour to appear as the victim. It does not necessarily follow, even if he is very much shaken in cross-examination, that the other side's version will be accepted and it is of course open to a judge not to give anything to either side.

In the event of your winning the case, I presume then that in order to be free, W. himself would afford you with evidence but he would also have to contribute a third of his income.

Yet another consideration is whether, if you stand firm, he is likely to make some compromise and offer settlement on the question of desertion right on the eve of the case. This is a possibility but I think a very doubtful one in view of the whole position of the lawyers. I think one should take it that the matter will now go forward unless any settlement is arrived at within the next few weeks.

As far as publicity is concerned, this is a matter which is greatly exaggerated as people forget very quickly what they read in the papers, and there is bound to be some sort of publicity now whatever occurs.

There is one further matter, which is the question of the costs which you have incurred and will incur with Gordon Dadds. My impression is that these are payable either by C. or W. whatever happens. I do know that Tilly had to pay a considerable sum to her solicitors . . .

Chapter IX

Lyall Street

In the Fifties, I lost three friends. The closest, Natalie Newhouse, affectionately known to her friends as Natalie Nuthouse, appeared to be either very self-destructive or a perpetual victim of disaster. She had once crashed through a skylight and, as the bone did not heal, had to spend months in plaster of Paris in a hospital. After a series of hapless love affairs, she married the actor, Robert Newton. The marriage was not a success. Her death was thought to be an accident. While in hospital once again, she was unwittingly given an overdose of sleeping pills.

An American girl, Angelica Weldon, after making several attempts at suicide, also finally succeeded by taking pills and, to make doubly sure of her fate, prepared a death chamber in her basement kitchen, turned on the gas and lay down beside the gas stove. Angelica had been having a long affair with Lady Aberconway's son, John Maclaren, a good-looking young man. Although one had always thought of him as being totally frivolous and superficial, he too, some weeks after Angelica's death, committed suicide by sealing himself in his garage, switching on the car engine to be asphyxiated by the fumes.

Marjorie Davenport also had suicidal tendencies. Once, John got home to find her unconscious in the bathtub, having slashed her wrists. Marjorie would get in touch with me when she was feeling depressed. I saw a lot of her the year before her death. Her worries seemed to be due to lack of funds and intensive household chores. When John went to Capri to visit Norman Douglas and her sons were at school, describing herself as a 'virtuous grass widow', Marjorie came to the country. She recounted how, the week before at a Bulgarian Legation dinner, as the ladies got up to go into the drawing room, her knickers had begun to slip. With one hand on her hip gripping them, she had had to dash up the stairs and knot them up on the landing — which I mention as it was so typical of her. Later, when I was about to drive down to the south of France, John came to see me to ask if I would take Marjorie with me. He had begun to weary of her gloomy moods and added, 'What's more, I don't care if she never comes back.' I had arranged to stay on the way in the Hérault with the painter Jean Hugo's wife, Lauretta, who replied to my telegram, 'Delighted to see you both'. In Paris, Marjorie and I shared a room in a hotel. Then we drove on to the Mas de Fourques and, after a few days, continued on to St Tropez. At this stage of the journey, even I began to find Marjorie difficult. As often happens with unhappy people, she became bitter and aggressive. One afternoon on the sands, seeing me applying varnish to my toenails, she accused me of being narcissistic and from then on began mooching off on her own, sometimes spending the entire night on the beach. Once, I came across her in the early hours doing a sensuous solo dance for the benefit of a steel band on the port.

When Cyril arrived from Hydra, where he had been staying with Joan Rayner and Paddy Leigh Fermor, we took her to lunch in Gassin. Then she disappeared. Back in London, Marjorie wrote describing her appalling journey in a crowded train, with no booked sleeper. She had spent most of the night in the corridor and when put in a carriage had had to sit bolt upright, afraid to lower her head and come into contact with a pair of smelly socked feet, though the Coca Cola boy in the corridor had offered to share his *couchette* and she rather wished she had accepted. John was not at home when she arrived, but he turned up in the early hours, a bit shaky after a roaring bachelor fortnight, very pleased to see her. The postcard she had sent giving the times of the train and boat had failed to reach him. 'Material situation unaltered . . . Prospects brightish . . . But no bird in the hand . . .' She had not yet had a bath because she could not bear to wash away all the sun and sea. 'This is the one and the most truthful way of thanking you, not for the b and b but for much nicer things. Much love from your dippy pal . . .'

A month later I was in Austria with W. I wrote saying how provincial and depressing I found Vienna, with the monotonous diet of goulash, the coffee with greasy blobs of cream and the highly coloured bottled raspberry juice that W. drank all the time, while exclaiming 'Very good, very good' to everything. Marjorie replied that she knew I would not have agreed with her about Austria, as I would be living at a more elegant level than she had been when there. The boys were home and the flat a shambles with meals, meals, meals galore. But John was on the wagon and in good form. They had just come from John's ex-wife's funeral at Golders Green Crematorium — the Welfare State's version of a Viking's funeral. It is a gentle Everglades, hygienic without cleanliness, *sans* life, *sans* death, *sans* everything. But the parson had taken elocution lessons, and afterwards in Camden Town they had bought the boys a grassnake that had already escaped from its cage three times and released its stink glands on everyone. 'I see you hanging on air,' she added, 'suspended between C. and W., rather in the manner of Blondin walking Niagara on a tightrope. Hail and farewell (I have not been drinking) Marjorie.'

The last letter was written from a ward in St Mary Abbot's Hospital. She had a busted ulcer, brought on after John had gone off to spend a week with friends in Dieppe. It happened on her birthday, when she had fainted in the King's Road. She was having dramatic midnight blood transfusions and was rather pleased with herself for achieving what she considered to be a good, healthy sort of ulcer, but depressed to think that she would have to remain in the ward at least another two weeks. 'It is so depressingly boring and gloomy here . . .' Would I please write, 'as it's so nice to get letters'.

Soon after, Marjorie jumped to her death from the top of the Strand Palace Hotel.

It was sad losing these three friends, though now I think that perhaps they were fortunate to have been spared old age, further loneliness and increasing disenchantment.

Some years back, Cyril and I had entrusted some meagre savings to Michael Becher, who was then a stockbroker. Michael invested unwisely. But when I left Chester Square and moved into Lyall Street, Michael refunded some of the money he had lost that, to his consternation (he probably assumed he was saving me from total penury), went on a carpet for the sitting room that contained nothing but a divan, a Danish dining table and four dining chairs. The flat never became entirely furnished. The bedroom was carpeted in blue with red curtains, the same sateen being draped round the bedhead and attached to the ceiling by a crown. Sutro provided the most up-to-date cooker. As I had no use for the two top-floor rooms, they were advertised in *The Times* and eventually became rented to a pair of budding actresses, one of them a German girl cut off from her family by Checkpoint Charlie. The girls were quiet, good tenants and always managed to pay their rent. I became a landlady.

Jocelyn Rickards lived in Lower Belgrave Street with John Osborne. I would walk to their house dressed in what John liked to described as 'my shelter clothes': a blue djellabah, a woolly shawl over a sheepskin-lined overcoat, under which I wore striped men's flannel pyjamas, a cashmere pullover and, for added warmth, thick, woolly socks and mittens. They would joke about my voracious appetite that often coincided with bouts of gloom. They identified me with the character in N. F. Simpson's play, *One-Way Pendulum*, who was employed to go round to people's houses and dispose of the leftovers in their fridges.

Jocelyn introduced me to the writer, Wolf Mankowitz. We hoped it might lead to a job. But after deploring the fact that I had let such a big fish as W. escape my net all he did was to give me the task of compiling a book of Jewish short stories. Most of them were so derivative that nothing came of the scheme.

A Co-Respondent hunt still being on, only the most intrepid gentlemen dared to be seen in my company. Alan Ross (editor of *The London Magazine*) would take me to Lords cricket ground, though I had never been able to appreciate cricket, even when I was a little girl and Daddy used to take me to watch the famous batsman, Jack Hobbs.

Alan had a passion for louche postcards, the kind you might find on the Brighton pier. They would be sent from Leeds or from wherever he had been to cover a cricket match that he then wrote up for *The Observer*. (1) A very made-up blonde with taloned shoes and a skirt up above her thighs is sitting on a couch, while a young man is about to put more coal on the fire: 'Before you do that, poke it up a bit,' she says. (2) The same blonde is seated on the lap of a red-faced, moustached colonel, and she says, 'Do you feel in the pink, Colonel?' 'Yes, if I can.' (3) A naked skeletal subaltern with a large, bushy moustache, clutching a towel round his parts, is having a check-up and the doctor says, 'I'm afraid you'll have to have it off, it's sapping your strength.'

Christmas 1957

Awoke to weather forecast. 'Fog patches will clear slowly during the morning, leaving a good deal of cloud. This evening cloud will thicken and there will be slight rain.' Alone for the first time for as long as I can remember. Cyril is spending Christmas with the Goldsmids. Not a word from Alan. After lunching with Gogi (whose husband, the film director, Lee Thompson, had left for Hollywood) I ran into Gerda's old *beau*, Goodley, in the street. Next day, Goodley came to lunch and Gogi to dinner. What a time! Afterwards, went to a party given by Leonard Rosoman and saw some new faces. Am quite vapid these days. Unless I take a pill awake each morning at four. It's as though an alarm goes off at that hour, leaving me tired for the rest of the day. W. has been seen with Nika Hulton's sister Elena, as related by Sutro. A saleswoman I have known for years has been questioned by detectives and subpoenaed. She was very nice about it, but the effect is always upsetting. We should be doing the same to W.; he would collapse at once. Let him think that Sonia or Caroline are giving evidence against him and it would work wonders.

Imagining he was doing me a good turn, Cyril got hold of some Serpasil pills. They were administered to wild animals to calm them while in transit from the jungle to a zoo. All they did for me was tempt me to emulate Marjorie.

'You must go on with them,' Cyril insisted. 'You have to feel far gloomier before you can reap any benefit.'

I cheered up the following spring when Alan took me to county cricket matches. And, one sunny day, we boarded a channel boat to see an exhibition of Mary Cassatt's paintings in the small Dieppe *musée*. As the boat was leaving Newhaven, three bulbous nuns in wimples appeared and stood conversing surreptitiously like spies on the *quai*. Alan exclaimed, 'Look! There's Cyril, Weidenfeld and Sutro.' From then on, whenever they cropped up in the conversation, they were jovially referred to as 'The Three Nuns'.*

'I've heard reports of some distasteful activities by Nun 1, relating to us and communicated (I understand unsuccessfully) to Nun 3,' Alan would say. From Australia, he wrote, 'This place like London is full of nuns. I shall be home tomorrow "nun" too soon.'

After spending a weekend with Nun 3 in the Quirinale Hotel in Rome, I joined Alan in Sicily. We visited Palermo, Syracuse, Taormina and Cefalu. One night, on arriving at one of the newly constructed Jolly Hotels, we found everyone had gone to bed. A night porter showed us to our rooms. Proud of his mastery of the lingo, Alan asked him to bring some *sapone*. We waited and waited, and were about to go to bed without any when a triumphant night waiter appeared hoisting a tray with two goblets of *zabaglione*, that delicious Italian dessert of Marsala wine, honey and egg yolks warmed over a *bain-marie*. Alan's comment was, 'They need to wash their ears out.'

When Alan flew off to Tunis, I was wandering round the Cefalu *musée* when a ragged young man wearing patched trousers and a threadbare jacket came up and asked if I had visited the *château*. He looked about twelve years old but claimed to be sixteen. He had large brown eyes and very white teeth, and was a very pretty boy when he smiled. From then on, every morning when I left the hotel, I found him awaiting me on the kerb. He took me to the Beasts House (Aleister Crowley) to see the reputedly erotic murals and into the hills where his brother tended a herd of goats, and helped me carry the luggage when I caught the train back to Rome. As a parting gift I gave him Alan's black pullover.

When Kenneth Tynan came to Lyall Street, he always joked about the stairs. All his current lady-friends, he said, inhabited top-floor flats, including Doris Lessing, to whose flat we went to a party one night. Tynan sometimes took me to lunch at the Ritz where I had had my last glimpse of Uncle Dudley,

---

* Three Nuns was a famous tobacco brand name at the time.

sitting amongst the palms, drinking tea with a group of friends, when he had become a stocky, Pickwickian figure and walked with the aid of a cane. It was after he had written to *The Sunday Times* to congratulate Cyril on getting a divorce, so we were not on speaking terms and merely peered at each other between the fronds.

When I mentioned to Kenneth that I felt sorry for Cyril – he seemed to be so unhappy – Tynan was shocked. You had to have contempt for someone you pitied. He linked love with *vedette* worship. To merit love you had to be glamorous. He always referred to Cyril as the 'Supreme Commander'.

'He won't do for you,' Cyril countered. 'You can divide people into ruminative or predatory types. We are ruminants. Tynan is predatory. He has the mentality of a journalist, always on the go. Elaine is not masochistic enough for him.' When I asked Kenneth what he felt about Elaine, he said, 'I couldn't bear a divorce. You see, I'm in love with her.' Then, realising he could not get away with that, he added hurriedly, 'That's ridiculous, I can't say that, but if she left me I'd kill her' – not himself, but her, as though she were an indispensible prop to his narcissistic ego. Talking of illegitimacy I said, 'It probably gives people more drive.' It hadn't applied to him, he said, he'd already had the drive before he knew. He compared our situation to the *Last of Chéri*. Even so, his two books were typically inscribed 'For Varvara Queen of the Big Top'.

From Tynan on, for several years it remained my fate not to be drawn to older people of either sex, as in the past, but to those far younger and you have to be a Lotte Lenya for that to work out.

When Sutro's chum, Ivan Moffat, came to lunch in Lyall Street, he said, 'You can't possibly remarry Cyril.' Ivan held a typically American attitude to marriage: to go back was defeat. You had to better yourself by marrying someone richer or more renowned. Just as later, when Kennedy was assassinated, a popular topic of conversation in New York was who can poor Jacky marry now? Until she came up with Onassis.

Cyril spent most of that year out of England, taking trips with the Hansi Lambert, staying with Joan and Paddy in Hydra or with Bill and Annie in their Perfectionist's Palace in Spain. When in London, he lodged in Percy Street, in Poppet's flat that she had let to the art critic, John Russell, whom Cyril dubbed 'one of nature's undertakers' because of his bedside wake at the demise of both Logan Pearsall-Smith and André Gide.

The cottage had been put into the hands of an estate agent and listed as 'Oak Tree Cot, a small, old-world cottage, pleasantly situated in lovely country with 1/3 acre of land'. Then the painter Michael Wishart wrote inviting me to Ramatuelle and I too slipped away. Cyril and I had once dined with the Wisharts in St Tropez, otherwise I hardly knew Michael, who was then separated from Ann. Cyril was not at all pleased when he learnt that I was in Ramatuelle. He wrote accusing me of shiftiness and deception. I replied that I had no reason to hide the fact and Ann also knew.

The South of France had already become a summer tourist trap. The tiny *place* of Ramatuelle was a vast parking lot with blaring radios, molten thighs, bare feet, bleached heads and gaping locals. Michael's walled house had faint privacy. Day and night couples tramped the alleys, or stood gazing up at the sumptuous, newly hung Wishart drapes. In the mornings, Michael drove off to work saying, 'I want to paint a little picture of a few crocus-coloured Medusas for you,' or he would come back and report that he was working on a 'big gold and lettuce-heart green painting redolent of Aragon'. If I was feeling energetic, I would walk down to St Tropez and meet him for dinner. In August, to escape the hordes, we drove to Spain and were joined by Cyril in Madrid. When he arrived in the Hotel Fenix, Cyril came up to the room and we ordered drinks. The three of us were about to go out to dinner, when Cyril noted that his wallet was missing. Then I remembered seeing the waiter bend over and pick up something from the foot of the bed. We complained to the management, but Cyril never recovered his pesetas or travellers cheques.

In his autobiography, *High Diver*, Wishart wrote, 'Cyril was in a very good mood, which is by no means always the case. Barbara enhanced his good humour by complaining about me, while I paid the bills . . .'

When Cyril got back to England he sent a *mandat*. From San Sebastian I wrote and thanked him, adding 'This is a very pretty place, it seems to have come to life since the Farouk trip. The bullfights are the best and I regret to say (don't be shocked) I am rather spellbound. Today, there were six, bad, tricky bulls; one jumped over the barricade immediately it got into the ring. Antonio Ordoñez was marvellous. Franco was there and Soraya, then divorced from the Shah of Iran, to whom Ordoñez dedicated a bad bull, which suddenly turned and spiked him in the left leg. He refused to have the wound dressed and did a perfect kill. Sorry to be such an enthusiast. Burgos is wonderful. The most beautiful town in Spain. Now don't be discouraged about your new house. You will make it very nice, have lots of friends in it and be very happy there. Michael sends his best wishes *et courage*, he enjoyed Madrid much more because you were there. Don't be unhappy, you wily old baby . . . B.'

Chapter X

'Whatever Are You Going To Do Now?'

Due to Cyril's fear of further publicity and my need to get over the whole Weidenfeld era, we finally agreed not to fight the divorce case. Sutro acted as my negotiator, with Marreco acting for W. Sutro hoped that finally he would be able to clinch the deal on desertion. In that way Cyril would not be implicated. So I wrote to Mr Pett of Gordon Dadds:

> It has now been decided to settle the case out of court and I have agreed to accept payment of £2,000, to be paid over a period of six years, with £400 down straightaway for this year. In return I withdraw my defence, but not until the covenant has been put through, of course. With regard to costs, Mr Weidenfeld pays his own (this must be guaranteed in writing) and Mr Connolly has agreed to pay mine as well as his own. Telephone me if you need to discuss anything. Today I am in bed with a lingering cold . . .

Mr Pett was sorry to hear I was in bed with a cold and wrote to say that it was, of course, for me to decide whether or not to fight my husband's case, but that I had obviously misconceived the position, if I hoped the case would be settled on desertion. For, if I withdrew my defence, W. would proceed and obtain a decree of judicial separation on the grounds of adultery:

> If he obtains his decree – as I think he is bound to do on an undefended case – he will, when the three-year period from the date of the marriage has expired, file a petition for divorce based on the same grounds as in his present petition.

Mr Pett added that he did not know who had been negotiating the arrangements, but to his mind a covenant such as I suggested might well be quite illegal and that we had better leave the matter open until I had fully recovered from my cold.

Next came a letter from W.'s solicitors, Theodore Goddard, to say:

Our client instructs us he will pay Peter Jones' account for £13.2.6d and the account of Phelps Beddard for £19.1.3d, which relates to some gift your client made to our client, and our client will instruct his servants to look into the question of the blue Bristol jug and the bottle of champagne.

Our client instructs us that his telephone account shows toll and trunk calls made during the period March 14 to June 17 while your client was in occupation of the house at Chester Square totalling about £20, and this too he will pay.

Gordon Dadds were cockahoop and they wrote, 'It seems there is a change of tactics on the part of your husband!' Adding:

We have succeeded in tying your husband into knots over the particulars of the petition. We obtained a further order from the registrar. Your husband appealed to the judge and although he was technically successful, the judge made an order which in the end was very little different from that of the registrar. These further particulars have not yet been delivered but, when they are, then I am afraid that at long last we must file your answer . . .

Which was the following:

We have had a further discussion with our client and have given her certain advice which she has accepted. We are therefore writing to inform you that our client has instructed us that she no longer wishes to deny the allegations contained in the petition.

Then I flew to Morocco to join Michael Wishart at the Grand Hôtel Villa de France, Tangier. '*Maison de premier ordre avec tradition et renommée depuis 80 ans, entourée d'un grand parc et terrasses, vue unique sur la Méditerranée et la Casbah.*' Typewriter left behind. Will one regret it? Usual discussion: what books should one have brought? I have taken a D. H. Lawrence and Wu Chieng-en's *Monkey*, translated from the Chinese by Arthur Waley. Will they be read? Very depressed and weepy, but then it often happens when taking pills. Am trying bromide as a calmative.

A strong wind and sunless. One goes into Dean's Bar and there is the old white-haired Negro, more doddery than ever, doling out tepid daiquiries. Poor old Dean. Takes me under his wing.

'Very smart, dear,' he says, 'I like you in black.'

Just keep wondering what I'm doing here. One tries to escape from oneself only to discover one's more embedded in the self than ever. I am cured of hashish. Easy to obtain but disgusting. M. keeps jubilantly repeating, 'I feel very remote, I feel more and more remote,' then becomes ashen and passes out.

Usual guilt about Cyril. Just burnt a hole in his cardigan from hashish ash. Mahraba Palace restaurant, boy dancer; delicious Pastella pie of pigeon, almonds, onions and fresh grapes cooked in oil and butter; marvellous Spanish prawns everywhere.

Agadir
February 19
Escaping from the wind in Tangier. Immediately discard all woollies. Sit in sun, cold thickens. M. says we're on a honeymoon. Worst meal yet at Hotel Saada. It's now full. On *demi-pension*. M. inclined to wake up querulous.

'Forgive me darling. It's because I love you that I'm like this. I care about every inflection of your pretty voice, there are so many ways you can hurt, you know.' Persistent twisting of forelock, picking of broken skin round fingernails, whistling 'Miss Otis Regrets' out of tune. 'Do you have to put sand in my eye? Or be so disagreeable, my darling? I live on the verge of panic and it doesn't take much to bring it out.'

After continual fussing over typewriter am lent a vast machine by a *garagiste*. Will it be used? *Monkey* remains unread. Lack of reading matter acute until I buy a François Mauriac novel and a French dictionary. Been away one week. It seems simply ages. Driven into irritable humour by M. persistently twirling his hair. He thinks the Arabs look hostile. Driving a nightmare because of potholes. On the top of a hill it's agoraphobia and at the bottom it's claustro. I awake with the feeling of a tight band clamped to my skull, my heart a sponge of despair; every time I catch my breath I release a jet of sadness.

Hôtel Saada, Agadir

Darling Cyril,

It's difficult to write as I am on the move. But when I get to the Mamounia perhaps you could telephone. It's a paradise of heat here. The sands are sublime, long virgin stretches, creamy breakers, and can paddle, but have a cold. Agadir has developed as a resort. But oh, the boredom of the evenings, with no good book. The fruit and flowers are a constant pleasure. We have hired a car at great expense, and although have been forbidden by the owner (because of bad roads) tomorrow we are setting off for Tafraout and Tiznit, then Mogador and Marrakesh. How I wish you were here. Very exciting birds everywhere, pure white cranes that roost on the parapets. The Moroccan wine just passable. The only unpleasantness: the police hammering on doors checking up on passports. If you want me to, I should like to spend a lot of time with you at Bushey, but not if it upsets your life at all. I always feel you are my rock, however many changes there may be. I hope you will remain so, even if it's only a dwindling one . . . I hope you are better now. This is just a hurried letter as M. is waiting in the bar. I miss you and love you very much, Barbara . . .

March 3, Hôtel des Iles Mogador, Essaouira
Up to now, this is the prettiest and cheapest place, deserving more than one star, compared with Tafraout, which gets three. It has the perfect blend of French Moroccan eighteenth-century architecture. The streets are broad, the houses white with blue shutters and beautiful portals. The Place de Gaulle is lined with pale barked trees like magnolias but which are, in fct, a species of fig. By the sea, an Edwardian-resort feeling; carriage loads of white-clothed, red-veiled Moroccan women, jangling with jewels, taking the air along the promenade with their pretty children with twisted top-knots, to which is pinned more jewellery. The hotel looks on to the sea; from my window I can see the islands and the tower with the cannons. Hardly any tourists come here. Moroccans loathe the French still and are intensely nationalistic. Hashish is forbidden, except for the old things who have been smoking it all their lives.

Hôtel Mamounia
I am reading *Alleys of Marrakesh* stolen from Dean's bar. Met Doan.
'When I get back to England I will send you some books,' I say.
'Send me yours,' he says.
'No, never,' I reply.
'Coquette,' 'you must not be so tense. Try to be more content with yourself. One must accept one's limitations. Live alone,' he counsels. 'It's good . . . solitude. Marriage is not for you. One has to compromise for marriage and you are not capable of it.'
'I love solitude during the day, but not in the evenings.'
'Well,' he laughs, 'if that is your reason for marrying . . . no wonder.' I laugh, too.
'Also, life seems so pointless alone.'
'Life is pointless,' he says, 'perhaps you need to suffer. A romantic. Yes?' He sighs: 'Ah! *Vous êtes trop compliqué pour moi.* What astrological sign are you?'
'Cancer. Both husbands were virgos. It's the worst possible *mélange*.'
'Why do you say that?'

'Because the stars say so.'

'Do you know what sign I am?'

'No.' Doan laughs.

'Virgo' he says.

In Marrakesh, Michael and I hardly saw each other. He went off alone on bus trips and when he got back in the hotel kept ringing up Anne.

'My poor little darling wife . . . having to have another baby . . . everything ghastly here . . . darling . . . are you listening? I don't specially want to live in England. You know what I like . . . working and seeing Francis . . . the room is pretty . . . if you were here we could sit out and drink white wine and eat smoked salmon. All the house part is out . . . ghastly squalid peeing Arabs . . . what there is of the country is so suburban . . . it's not what you or I like, more and more money for more and more boredom. And don't think Marrakesh is beautiful . . . tawdry mountains . . . hideous and expensive . . . it has a reputation for being marvellous, I know . . . well, like your husband, but it doesn't live up to it. [Michael laughs] And last night I was so sort of sad that I got wildly drunk and still am . . . well, yes, [impatiently] are you listening? I don't specially want to live in England . . . all the things I detest visually . . . here . . . the worst disappointment I've ever had . . . it's never really sunny . . . when it's sunny a filthy wind and ghastly English everywhere . . . you were right, darling, to *think I could have spent the money on a Thunderbird.*'

Chapter XI

Flight

When I got back to England Cyril took me to Bushey Lodge, the house not far from Lewes that he had rented on Lord Gage's estate. His Lordship was a charmingly innocuous gentleman we termed the 'Intelligence Gauge'. Perhaps unwisely, Cyril sought my advice on distempering. I then had a passion for violent tints. The last time the cottage had received a coat of paint, the colours were so garish that the overall effect had been reminiscent of a Neapolitan icecream. Bright orange was chosen for the dining-room walls of Bushey to meld with the pretty brick tiles. I was never to live there, though, for by then Cyril had fallen in love with Deirdre. I did go down at weekends. Once, a neighbouring couple came to dinner. The husband had some interest in the Mermaid Theatre and used his influence to get me engaged as secretary to one of the directors. As anyone who has experienced one, let alone two, divorces, in rapid succession may understand, I was still demoralised and it turned out to be a particularly depressing interlude, due to the long Tube journey and the area in which the Mermaid was situated. I never glimpsed a director and sat about most of the day with nothing to do. I was entitled to free tickets, though, and a very good production of Brecht's *Galileo* was playing at the time.

In spite of a crushing survey – 'old timbers supporting beams in bad state . . . dampness in back and side walls of weather boarding in bad shape . . . crack down sitting-room wall . . . slats upon which the tiles are hung rotten . . . joists supporting beams riddled with worm . . . a complete new stack pipe and damper required' – the cottage was sold without regret for £2,000. I had had her for twenty years. When candles and Aladdin lamps had been replaced by electricity, she lost a lot of her charm. Also, during our absence, a dishonest gardener had dug up all the crocus, daffodil and narcissus bulbs that had festooned the grass and given us so much pleasure in the spring. I don't think I could ever have lived there again. The surroundings would always have been associated with Cyril. He inherited my old double bed and various other relics, as well as 'the little bus', as we used to call the Sunbeam Talbot. In later years, during any subsequent sentimental visits we paid the area, we found nothing had changed. Elmstead Church remained just as desolate, the branches of the yew tree supported by ropes. There was still the same three-forked signpost indicating the way to Canterbury, Hythe and Wye, and the cottage dormer windows still looked out across an expanse of unspoilt countryside.

On our last jaunt together, Michael and I visited Corsica. We took the ferry to Ile Rousse and stayed in the Hotel Napoleon Bonaparte. This was before the island had been invaded by French Algerians known as *pieds-noirs*. In the Sixties, when Algeria gained her independence, many of these families took up residence in Corsica and enriched the island by building reservoirs and planting vineyards. But when we drove round, it was completely deserted. Lush meadows were covered in wild flowers and the hedgerows were a mass of honeysuckle, arbutus and dog roses; the interior of the island was desolate *maquis* with an occasional valley and banana grove. The villages had become tumbledown ruins inhabited by septuagenarians or folk deformed from inter-breeding, rather like the little people one might see in a Buñuel film. The young had departed to seek employment on the Continent. Restaurants, bordering the sea, served delicious *langoustes* and real mayonnaise, and in the evenings sparkling fireflies hovered about our drinks.

Behind Ile Rousse was the hill village of Monticelli. We drove up one evening just as the shepherd, followed by his flock, was coming down the mountain to the chime of goat bells. It was such an enchanting, pastoral scene that after seeing a notice, 'A Vendre', on a ruined house, with a view of the sea from the upstairs windows and a large garden dominated by a tombstone, I called on the *notaire* of Ile Rousse, M. Fiovanti, the following day and made an offer. He said the house was owned by a family of twelve and every member would have to sign the *Acte de Vente*. He would contact me as soon as he had traced them all. I left an advance of 865,000 (old) francs and returned to Lyle Street. Weeks went by without any news. The following spring I returned to Ile Rousse, seen off at Newhaven by Cyril and Stephen Spender, who kindly wrote a note to the Baron Henri de La Grange: 'This is to introduce my friend, Barbara Skelton. Please show her the delights of Calvi.' I telephoned and was invited over for a drink. There were no buses going to Calvi, so I had to hitch. In spite of the distance, that was no problem. Corsicans, then, at any rate, were far more forthcoming than drivers on the Continent.

The Baron's house stood on the corner of a charming old cobbled *place*. I rang the bell, and a man took me into the sitting room and offered me a drink. Then he disappeared, while from upstairs came the sound of someone playing the piano. I was left alone shyly to sip my drink and read the book that, luckily, I had taken with me, when an elegant woman put her head round the door. She too disappeared. Then, suddenly, there was a stampede on the stairs and a man called out, 'We're all going to dine out in a restaurant.' And out they all trooped, leaving me to gather up my basket and hitch back in the dark to Ile Rousse.

Later, rumours of the visit drifted back. The Baron and his friends had assumed me to be a secretary on *Encounter* and therefore, it seems, socially *infra dig*!

Back in London, I found a letter from Doan to say he was *'dans l'effervescense du départ pour l'Angleterre'*, having been invited to stay *'par une délicieuse vieille dame, Lady Astor'*, and that he was leaving for Casablanca and would arrive in London in about a week. He had also been invited by Mrs Diana Campbell-Gray to make a tour of *'Ecosse: délicieuse idée!'* And when would we meet? He had received the copy of *The Unquiet Grave; 'très, très intéressant. Je regrette de ne pas posséder la langue anglaise pour apprécier le texte dans toutes ses finesses. Je pense à vous, mes meilleurs souvenirs à Cyril.'*

When we met in London, I sought Doan's advice on the Monticelli affair: he said he knew of a Moroccan astrologist; I was to give him the date and the time of day that I had first seen the house, together with its situation, and when he got back home he would get its horoscope taken. Michael was in London and called me saying, 'Darling girl', he had had two *amours* since we had parted but 'neither paddles in the shallow end of the pale pool of love had dimmed for one moment' my 'most loved aura of delight and boy's brain'. His current lady friend had said that life was inventing a series of excuses not to die, 'and lucky you, you have Monticelli!' He said that he often nearly died in his night- and daydreams, when he envisaged my delicious Egyptian cat face close up and that embracing me had been like embracing a river or a ribbon, and that he was going to show me his latest painting of a rainbow trout, 'like the one we saw together in the Ajaccio market'.

A month later, Doan wrote from the Derb el Hanch in Marrakesh to say that he didn't have very good news: my horoscope was all wrong, particularly with regard to 'places of refuge'; I would have nothing but problems. Every sentence in the letter ended in *'changement peu favorable'*, *'vous aurez des ennuis'*; then finally, *'J'espère, chère Barbara, que vous me répondrez, car je suis très curieux de savoir la suite de cette affaire.'* I wrote to the *notaire* demanding a refund. Months went by and no news, so Pierre Sauvaigo, a respected Niçoise lawyer, interceded in the matter. Eventually, I flew over to France and claimed the money in cash from a Paris bank.

As soon as I arrived back, feeling hungry, I went to the Express Dairy and bought some eggs. Tired after the hurried journey, the suitcase unpacked, the room in disorder, the residue of the Monticelli ruin resting on the mantle, I lay down on the bed in my old red dressing gown and dozed. I was awakened by a board creaking in the passage, then very furtively the bedroom door opened, held by a black-gloved hand, and a strange man's face peered into the bedroom. I lay perfectly still without moving my head and looked at him as he looked at me. Then the bedroom door closed as slowly and furtively as it had opened, and the stranger fled. The doorbell was out of order, so he must have rung and, getting no reply, assumed the flat to be empty. The front door had been forced with a jemmy. I dialled 999. In no time, a plainclothes policeman with mediocre good looks, wearing a duffle coat, walked in carrying what looked like a toolbox. Once in the bedroom, he looked baffled and stared at me as if awaiting an explanation. He said he had come to take fingerprints.

'He wore gloves,' I said.

'Oh well then, it's not worth it. Did he steal anything?'

'No, although I can't think why he didn't take the portable radio from the next room.'

'I suppose he was looking for jewellery. Do you have any?' I thought no more about it. A week later he telephoned to ask if it would be convenient to see me right away. I took him into the sitting room and asked if he would like a drink. To my surprise, he accepted a large gin. Then he produced a portfolio of criminals, but none of the faces corresponded to the man I had seen and, in any event, I don't believe that after such an interval anyone would have been able to identify a strange face.

The detective-inspector became a regular visitor. He rang practically every day or came round to the flat, either in the morning or afternoon, never in the evening, when he had to get back to his steak, he said, and, I assumed, his wife, though he always denied having one. Sometimes, as soon as he entered the door, he would pick me up and twirl me round in his arms, as one might do with a doll.

'I like bringing someone of your intelligence down to my level,' he would say. Or, 'Sex is a great leveller.'

If I had been up at three in the morning making bread and milk, 'You're suffering from night starvation.' Another time, 'You're very maternal, aren't you?'

'Yes,' I said, 'I hope it doesn't irritate you.'

'Oh no'; he was most decisive. 'I like to be babied.'

Should I appear unfriendly, probably because he had not come round the previous day, 'Is the novelty wearing off?' he would ask. One afternoon, very troubled, he said, 'It worries me taking off my trousers. I keep imagining the boss coming in.' Happily, when he announced how much he would like to be 'my protector in the park' I was already planning to visit the United States.

Diary

January 2 1960

I really am going to keep a diary throughout this year. Have been too despairing and lazy during the last. I think I am completely out of the wood. Have got over the shock and demoralisation resulting from Cyril's marriage to Deirdre. Am almost content. The short spell of John Raymond served some purpose. He was clearly very devoted, without it being founded on much.

'You're really an extraordinary woman. Nothing but gaiety, chivalry, charm and wit ... etc. Bless you. But I'll go out of your life without fuss. I promise you. I'm very drunk, I know that, and very *happy*. I apologise for that, too. I know I'm very drunk but I was feeling rather lonely and loused up ...'

Last night he got the brush-off. A sentimental softie. A masochistic blubberer with outbursts of violent aggression towards the nearest victim. And, if one retaliates, he runs.

January 14

Today Cyril's baby was born. He said if it had not been born prematurely it would have been an Aquarius. He rings up at six in the evening, talks in breathless tones. 'How is the baby?' I ask. 'Fetching,' he says. 'Like some delicious animal in Harrods pet shop. It made a kind of squeak, has red hair and its eyes are closed.' Said he had never seen a new born baby before, and he had been afraid he might be repelled. Asks how I like the scarf he had bought me from Turnbull and Asser. I said it was very pretty. 'If you like it,' he added, 'I will get another of the same design, only in a different colour, to have one like yours.' Already, the sentimental words of a pending separation. Collect new passport photographs. Wash hair ... feel frostbitten, wretched and alone.

The week before my departure to the States, a locksmith came to repair the front door. I was vaccinated. I lunched with Mummy and the next day took a train to Brighton to have a final lunch with Cyril at the Mad Mascot. After lunch we drove along the coast past a daisy-chain of bungalows to Eastbourne and ordered tea in the Grand Hotel, while an orchestra played extracts from *Gigi*. The night before my departure, Cyril came round to the flat with Peter Quennell. When he learnt that I intended to spend four months in the States on $1,000, Peter exclaimed, 'That'll last you a couple of weeks.' Cyril, who was used to me terminating letters, 'From your thrifty wife', merely smirked.

'Perhaps a bit longer. You're so careful.'

'I hope your marriage will work out,' I said.

'Oh yes,' Cyril was definite. 'The baby will cement it.'

The last person to telephone was the detective-inspector. Was I really leaving? He sounded offhand. Perhaps the boss was in the room. Then on March 12, Sutro took me to the airport. Once above the cloud fleeces, I felt almost carefree and euphoric.

Doan

Alan Ross

George Weidenfeld

Natalie Newhouse

Poppet

Me in Spain

Cyril and Alan Ross

Michael Wishart

Wirra

Tantine

Didessa

Folie and Mell

With Bob Silvers in Westhampton

Jane Sprague in Westhampton

Me in New York

Marjorie Davenport

Alastair Hamilton in Mexico

Charles Addams

The *mas*

Bernard Frank

At my present home

Chapter XII

New York

Gerda lived on 57th Street, in what she termed 'her pad' – an apartment crammed not only with her knick knacks, but those of the previous tenant, horse prints of hunters straddling a brushwood fence, china dogs and cats moulded in sentimental poses, ornamental bowls filled with peanuts and potato chips, black lacquer tables and frilly lampshades like large picture hats, all of which created the atmosphere of a cosy jumble sale. The drinks tray was on a black trolley and beside an array of glasses stood a passable bottle of brandy, Californian wine and gin in what looked like detergent bottles. With her large blue eyes, pale skin and long blonde hair, which she pinned back in a *chignon*, Gerda was still beautiful. The only giveaway was the loose, wrinkled flesh of her neck, accentuated by the tight pearls she wore with a plain black, *décolleté* dress. She had been in her thirties when she emigrated to the States, with practically no money, after paying to get a divorce from her stockbroker husband, Ronny Simmons. The pearls, she said, had been a present, not from her second husband, Roger Treat, a sportswriter who lived in their country house in Connecticut where Gerda spent weekends, but from someone she referred to as her 'man', who was loaded. He owned a house on the East Side and a beach house on Long Island. She had known him for a year, but he was not particularly generous. She loved her pearls. She had had to ask for them, though, Gerda said. Before that, all he had given her was some worthless gift like a Chibachi grill, picked up on one of his European trips. Apparently, he also had a wife and they were about to divorce.

'I'm going to wait until she gets up off her arse and goes to Reno,' Gerda said. She drew the curtain and the sudden draught caused little black particles of dust to scurry across the ledge, but as soon as the window was closed, one no longer heard the expiring gasps of the buses which halted at the lights opposite. Then she let down her hair, peeled off her dress and overshoes, and put on Chinese slippers and a Bloomingdale housecoat, one of the many hanging in the cramped bathroom. Nearly everything she possessed seemed to have been bought in duplicate. The icebox was crammed with cracker barrel cheese, natural caraway, Kraft 'Natural Swiss' and 'Natural Colby', cooked roast beef and gravy, Coney Island french fries, peach pies, apples pies and all-batter chocolate brownies.

It was over ten years since we had seen each other and Gerda had become totally Americanised. The cupboard a 'walk-in-closet', women were 'broads', penises 'drinkles'; anything she didn't like was 'for the birds'. Although she had to rise early to get to First and 58th, where she supervised the Revlon Beauty Salon, we hardly slept the first night. Talking of some celebrity, Gerda said, 'I've made up her kisser many a time.' I complimented her on her looks. She had to wear a girdle now, though.

'When you've reached my time of life, you can't have an arse floating about like a jelly,' she said.

Next day it snowed and when I went out, snowflakes had settled on the awnings. In spite of the smell of centrally-heated fry and the look of the men with their brutish, Neanderthal heads, I immediately fell in love with Third Avenue. The smuggler, Toot, whom I had last seen on the Côte d'Azur, was also in New York, training for an American flying licence. After being imprisoned in Shanghai for smuggling gold, he had decided to go straight. Old Bill was there working for Shell. He was so disparaging when he spoke of the New Yorkers that he was labelled 'the good-will Ambassador'. I would meet them in Roger's on Lexington. It did not take long to discover that even in the scruffiest bar, one of the main pleasures of New York was the drinks, whether it were gallons of 100% pure, unsweetened King Sun fruit juice (which caused one's breasts to swell), Rob Roys (a Martini made with scotch), Red Snappers (bloody mary made with gin) — named after a Florida fish — or whisky sours drunk in the bar of the St Regis. But after hearing many a joyous waiter's peel of 'another dago red here', I became wary of ordering wine. Gerda always knew when I had been into Roger's. Sniffing me, she would say, 'You've been in that terrible dump again. Go clean yourself up, kid.'

One soon got used to seeing large groups of women being escorted to the most prominent table in a restaurant, all of them wearing identical little black dresses and six-tiered ropes of peals. Old B. took me to a fish restaurant on Third and kept sending the waiter off to get something or remove the iceberg lettuce that accompanied each dish.

'You think we're fussy, don't you?' he said. The waiter was not at all perturbed.

'Oh no,' he replied, 'I think you're interesting. I don't have the same experience as you do. But I'd like to.'

Once I had made contact with the introductions I had brought from England, there was never a dull evening. Describing her as being 'a wild-living honey round forty, (divorced)', as though announcing a trade, Tynan had provided Dorothy Biddle's telephone number. She was looking for someone to share her apartment on Fifth Avenue and invited me for drinks. All her friends wore superb fur coats and one of them was even dressed in panther skins, but it soon became clear to Dotty that I would be a wash-out as a tenant.

Sutro had given me an introduction to Anita Loos, author of *Gentlemen Prefer Blondes*, who invited me to tea. As Sutro was in the movie business, she assumed me to be an actress. The following day, a man rang to offer me a part in a forthcoming musical. Sutro's aunt invited me to dinner and a concert in Carnegie Hall. I also had a little black Mattli dress on to which I had pinned the Farouk clip. Aghast when she saw it, she begged me not to be seen wearing such an ostentatious jewel in the street.

Stephen's introductions were the most rewarding. Unlike the Baron de La Grange, Chuck Turner, also a musician, became a close friend, as well as the bright, witty and ambitious Earl Macgrath, then secretary to the composer, Gian Carlo Menotti, and both of them put me up in their apartments. Chuck's attic apartment had a view on one side of the 59th Street bridge, with cars racing over it and, on the other, a consolidated laundry. Chuck loved concocting odd dishes and suffered from intermittent bulimia. One evening, he was preparing a dinner for some friends, amongst them the composer Samuel Barber, with whom for many years Chuck had lived. The *gigot* being *cuit*, Chuck opened the oven and a swarm of cockroaches ran out. These little monsters thrive all over the States.

The only hopeless introductions had been provided by Peggy Guggenheim – a few choice words written on the thinnest of rice paper to gallery owners, none of whom responded. The Tynans, however, were in New York. Elaine arranged a luncheon in Le Bistro on Third and 49th, one of those small, intimate, pseudo-French restaurants that abound in New York. We were a party of six, including the two most sought-after about-town bachelors of that period: Bob Silvers, then editor on *Harper's*, and the *New Yorker* cartoonist Charles Addams. It was clever of Elaine, for Don Juan Silvers and Charlie Casanova became regular escorts. As we left Le Bistro, the latter invited me to lunch the next day in the Rainbow Room, at the top of the Waldorf. Then he took me to Long Island. We drove there in his Bentley. Charlie had a passion for vintage cars. There was also an old Bugatti in the garage, where he would spend hours tinkering and cranking to get her to start, a moment I dreaded, for we would then go for a bump full speed round Westhampton. Charlie's little clapboard house, situated on an inlet of the sea, was a veritable folly. His Chriscraft was moored at the end of a jetty. In the summer, when we sat on the terrace drinking, yachts sailed by. Many yacht owners knew Charlie. There would suddenly be a shout of 'Hoi, there!' and an exchange of greetings.

Charlie made excellent Martinis. On my first visit, I drank so many that I became very aggressive and accused him of being 'mean', 'a rotten lecher', 'vain' and 'selfish'. The following day, we drove at full speed back to New York, where I was dropped off on the kerb with a serpenty kiss and the words, 'Call you next week'. I spent that Sunday alone with a drainpipe for company.

On the next visit, I called him an 'American Blimp' and a 'tin hoarder'. When we returned to New York, it was no longer 'I'll call you' but 'Call me'. Even so, he rang soon after and took me to a farewell party the Tynans were giving. When he introduced me to James Thurber, then totally blind, Thurber groped for my hand and murmured, 'Hallo, darling'. Afterwards, we went to the 21 Club. It was a stiflingly hot evening. Even so, most women were swathed in tippets. At the next table, amongst a group of six, was a fleshy brunette who sat with her elbows resting on coasters and her head buried in her hands. Suddenly, she jerked her face to one side and threw up over her shoulder. Her companions seemed not to notice, but within seconds, a little bellhop appeared with a sick pail and broom.

Charlie was, on the whole, a passive man, with immense charm and a most appealing way of moving, in a kind of swinging gait. As well as vintage cars, he collected medieval bows and arrows that were attached to the walls like paintings. In the sitting room, there were also a medieval coat of armour and a canary bird that flew out of its cage at drinks time. He was not at all loquacious, but his remarks could be as humorous as his cartoons. Once, driving back from Long Island, as we were passing the crammed cemetery, he remarked, 'They must be standing up in there.' Another time, when I went to his apartment for dinner, he was praising some book and, as though addressing a total philistine, I said, 'But, I've never seen you reading.' Topping up my drink, he said, 'Do you expect me to sit here and read in front of you?'

I always loved being taken to Gerda's white clapboard bungalow on the edge of a lake surrounded by a forest of dogwood trees in Connecticut. Sometimes, we swam in the lake and the neighbour's freshly fished trout tasted simply delicious. It was only when I became totally infatuated with the elusive Charlie that the lake symbolised death.

Gerda's husband, Roger, was a reformed alcoholic. In his late forties, he remained strangely infantile.

'Where's my cud?' he would say – short for cuddly – a blanket. He took me to AA meetings that were far from dull, when the 'alkies', as he called them, got up and confessed to the degrading acts they had committed in order to obtain more booze. In general, though, New Yorkers are reticent about drinking. If someone has a bad hangover, he never says so, but, 'I woke up feeling rather tired today.'

Roger had just written a novel that his publishers had given a boost in *Time*. Most of the women characters were depicted as whores; they were all in for it and, on practically every page, 'Her breath quickened' or 'He kissed her on the mouth hard' or 'Peter, that's lovely. It makes me all – you know. Is there more?' Sometimes when Gerda went back to New York, I would stay on in Newtown and return by rail. The trains were very slow and dirty. Once I was sitting next to a girl in the dining car who exclaimed, 'Just look at that waiter's jacket! One doesn't come in here to be nauseated, after all.'

Americans are always ready to converse and ask personal questions. Once, I returned on the bus and the driver managed to keep up a conversation all the way into New York, his eye on my reflection in the mirror above his head, while dogwood trees, streams, lakes and waterfalls flashed past.

'You really were dreaming when I drove up,' he started off by saying.

'I was told your bus would be late.'

'But it wasn't, was it?' Pointing to the scenery, he said, 'The more you see of the world, the more you want to run into the woods!' After listing all the Asian countries he had been to, he said he wanted very much to visit England, especially Ireland. 'People think I am Irish, but I don't look it. At least, I don't think I do.' He was very interested in religion and was planning to spend his vacation with the Shakers, a sect similar to the Quakers. They believed in complete segregation of the sexes. Was I 'Protestant? Episcopal? Congregational? Methodist?' Being ignorant of the distinctions, I said, 'Episcopal.' Did he go to church regularly?

'I haven't been for months. I feel ashamed. But, you know', he said, 'it may sound silly, but when I've been to church I always have better luck.' Talking of New York, 'I wouldn't give you a nickel for it. Dog eatin' dog.' The Puerto Ricans were more desperate than the Negroes. 'And when they intermarry they're not liked by either side. They have illegitimate children, live on relief, have TV, drink beer and don't work. They're filthy – their minds too.' And so it went on until the skyscrapers loomed on the horizon.

When not staying with Gerda, I went from pillar to post, sleeping on a let-down couch next to hissing hot pipes, an open suitcase by my side, to be awoken by a voice saying, 'What about a little symphonette for breakfast?' And on would go *Gigi*, for it was all the rage, at the time.

The first party I went to was given by Dwight Macdonald, founder and editor of *Politics Literary Review*. He was an anarchist, a life-long friend of Mary

McCarthy and could be very pedantic when drunk. When I entered, Mary's ex-husband, Bowden Broadwater, said, 'Come and meet the VIPs' and steered me across the room to talk to John Russell's first wife, Vera, who turned her back. John Rushole (Russell) was sitting on the edge of his chair and whispered, 'Where are you staying?' Bowden was very adept at making snide remarks which, alas, one couldn't always catch, as they were hissed out of the corner of his mouth. Caroline was there, with her husband, Israel Citkovitz.

'I don't care much for Macdonald,' I said. 'He's like an overgrown boy scout. Or his wife, for that matter.'

'Just wait until you meet Mrs Trilling', she replied. Her husband, Lionel Trilling, was a writer who taught English literature at Columbia University and they were both very intellectual. William Phillips, co-founder with Philip Rahv of the *Partisan Review*, asked me what class I belonged to.

'None really,' I said. 'If anything, middle.'

'How you must wish to be upper,' was his response.

When I said I was going to Boston for the weekend, to see Edmund Wilson, Phillips instantly had to let me know that he too was going away, not only this weekend, but the following one too. He came straight out of the status book. Phillips was planning to go to England. He would ring me up practically every day in a great fret about his reception there. I wrote to Cyril saying what a dismal little snob he was:

He showed me a sucking-up letter he had written to you and I advised him to cut it down, for the ingratiation went on for pages. Although he appears to be thoroughly nice, he has a reputation for being a creep and is not at all popular. He was about the only person not invited to the Tynan farewell. Both Caroline and I think him dismally stupid; he only rings up if he wants something and has not asked me to a single thing, so I don't think you need feel obliged to entertain him too lavishly. I have just been to see the Edmund Wilsons. I like her very much, but found it a bit sticky. I think he was quite astounded by my ignorance. The Mrs took me to Salem. It was sunny. There are some ravishingly pretty clapboard houses with Palladian windows painted dark grey and the magnolias were in full bloom. Otherwise, I sat on the banks of the Charles River with a book most of the time.

Cyril replied:

Just got your sweet letter and very pleased with it. I have just had lunch with PQ and given him your address. He is coming to NY in a week I think and is very anxious to see you. He has promised to ask his publishers, the Viking Press, if they can give you some reading — it seems to me the *easiest* job for you is to read MSS in your own time and comment on them and make suggestions. Anyhow, you can at least talk it over with him and he is very well disposed and liked you very much the last time he saw you. No real news for you as I have been buried in work. I retire into it now like Kupy* into the bottom of your bed and find the inside of a book the only place where I feel safe, or I sit through the marvellous afternoons of early summer in the gloomy junk room of the cottage fiddling with old bank statements, telegrams, corrected proofs and worthless articles: what a punishment. I see from your old letters that the bad thing about our marriage was that you had so much contempt for me. By the time we got married most of the love had gone and I was a husband. A figure of fun, know all, humbug, bald patch, quota peg, circumference and so on. There seemed to be something in you which hated a husband and took everything good about one for granted, concentrating on the faults. I see that the alternative of remaining married to you and waiting for W. to blow over would never really have worked because your contempt for me would be increased and so you would have always been looking for someone else – this does not mean that I do not feel terribly sad about the whole thing, particularly about what has happened since, but I don't believe we could have come together without a divorce. We were pretty washed up when we went to Greece together. I found on looking through all this muck that I really have only loved you and Jean – everybody else seems to have been part of an hallucination – as Siegfried loved Gutruna after swallowing the philtre. We should have got going at Bedford Square when we were both less suspicious. It has been wonderful, the last few days, the colour of sea and downs, the new leaves, the sunshine. It is a great happiness to go out in the little bus, open again, making its merry song or 'bark', as the sportscar enthusiasts call it.

The baby has begun to laugh and takes more interest in things. I do hope she is an intelligent, cheerful, positive character and not an elfin waif. She seems robust so far. At the moment D. has whisked her off to Lewes after announcing that our marriage is finished as I obviously prefer you . . . she saw that I was carrying your letter about in my wallet which I do because I can never remember your address. A Freudian lapse. I have heard very little news as am too broke to see anyone. My *Pavillons* are finished and the bank manager and income-tax man are waiting with their tongues hanging out for the cheque. I hope there will soon be something for you, i.e., some magazine rights or something. Have also done a piece for the *ST* on the

---

* Kupy was a coati-mundi who shared my life with Cyril at the Cot before being given to the zoo at Ilfracombe (see *Tears Before Bedtime*).

beginnings of modern poetry (Eliot, Yeats and Pound). I feel I have not a moment to waste and must be working all the time or I shall leave chaos behind. Saw Michael Wishart and Nicky at Janetta's. They look a completely happy queer couple or at any rate self-sufficient and were going off on a skiing holiday in Switzerland. The John Russells are getting Clive Bell, who is ill, to go and live with them. Isn't it extraordinary after Logan Pearsall-Smith, Matthew Smith etc?* They only take terminal cases! My heart bleeds for you and I will help you as soon as I can.

You were lucky to be away for the royal wedding. There has never been so much pointless mobbing and hysteria and endless yak yak yak *'pour l'accouplement de deux nains'*.

In case I stop this letter now, this is just to say that I long for your letters, that I want to hear about everyone, that I love you and miss you desperately, but want you to enjoy yourself. I think you should plan to get back to the Mediterranean now rather than summer in the US . . .

I then received a letter from the lawyers to say: 'We have filed a divorce petition against you on the part of your husband and enclose the following documents . . .' One headed 'In The High Court of Justice Probate Divorce' said:

TAKE NOTICE that a Petition has been presented by Arthur George Weidenfeld. If you do not intend to answer the charges, nor to be heard on the other claims in the Petition you need not do anything more than send the Form of Acknowledgment of Service. The Court may then, without further notice from you, proceed to hear the Petition and pronounce judgment, notwithstanding your absence . . .

Clause 5 of the Petition read, 'The Respondent has frequently committed adultery with the said Cyril Connolly . . .' and Clause 6, 'The Petitioner has not in any way condoned or connived or been accessory to the said adultery and therefore the Petitioner prays the said marriage may be dissolved, and that the Co-Respondent be condemned in the costs of this suit . . .'

The Petitioner's prayers were answered and I wrote to Cyril, 'The W. Petition arrived yesterday. Without reading it all, I just signed whatever it was and posted the form into the nearest box, stampless, what's more. I won't have enough money to go west and don't really care. I don't like travelling alone here. The evenings are so sad.'

---

* Matthew Smith was a painter.

In July, I flew back to London. The telephone was ringing as I entered the flat. It was Cyril. Soon after, I ran into Lee Miller, then married to Roland Penrose, who intoned, 'Whatever are you going to do now, Barbara?' When I saw Jocelyn she had an American model girl staying with her and whenever I went round to dinner, Jane Sprague would be laying the table, dressed in a T-shirt and black tights, which gave the impression she was out to vamp John Osborne. Jane was exceedingly tall with superb legs, blue-grey eyes and bobbed white hair, and had been briefly married to a French count. In order to obtain a British work permit she then married an Armenian, Steve, and soon got tired of him, whereupon Steve fell in love with her and became so violently jealous that she sought refuge with Jocelyn.

One evening, the fashion photographer, Alec Murray, came to dinner. Though he only lived round the corner, he arrived in a Citroën, bringing two dachshunds. Suddenly, the downstairs doorbell rang. We looked out of the window and there was Steve. Knowing Alec to be a close friend of Jane and seeing his car outside, Steve had assumed that Jane was with us. I had never met the Armenian gentleman and saw no reason to answer the insistent peel of the bell. Dinner over, we looked out again and there was Steve, as Alec said, 'pissed as a newt', busily puncturing Alec's tyres. The following day, I received a bouquet and a note of apology. Soon after, Jane moved into Lyle Street and slept on the divan in the sitting room. Appearances mattered a great deal to her. If, like her, you were not impeccably dressed, she was embarrassed to be seen in your company and, when in the street, would walk a few paces ahead, disowning one, so to speak. I reacted badly to this quirkiness as, at that time, I seemed to be deliberately looking my worst; in Jane's company the hem of a skirt would become mysteriously unstitched and I even found myself entering a cinema wearing carpet slippers. Even so, we maintained an amicable relationship. Then one day Jane, disillusioned with marriage, and I, disillusioned with life in general, booked a double cabin on the *Liberté*. This time I planned to remain in New York. The flat was rented to the American poet, Theodore Roethke, and his wife, Beatrice, then the two ageing *femmes fatales* were seen off early one November morning at Victoria Station by Jocelyn, Cyril and John Osborne. We had a very rough voyage, almost the last for the *Liberté*; soon after she was scrapped. Another passenger in the second class was a folk-singing pupil of Woody Guthrie, who haunted the decks dressed as a cowboy, nursing a guitar. He made Jane rock with laughter by saying I resembled Churchill. When we docked in New York, Cowboy helped with the luggage and we taxied to Gerda, who instantly took a dislike to Cowboy's hat and kept saying, 'Why don't you have a haircut?'

The following day, I moved into the Pickwick Arms Hotel on 51st. After signing in, I moved towards the lift followed by Cowboy, who was helping me carry the luggage, when the lady at the desk shouted, 'Now then, none of that! No gentlemen allowed upstairs.' The hotel was cheap and clean. I remained cooped in the space of a cupboard until, with Charlie's help, I found an apartment on 54th Street.

Darling Cyril,

I have now moved into a nauseous apartment costing $160 a month, which includes everything but the telephone. Nothing in it yet but the teachests, a camp bed and two throwouts (a painted desk and black-lacquered table of Mr A). For any less here, rooms are really squalid; also people seem to take a ridiculously probing interest in location. It means that after the Roethke rent I have to find $30. I sobbed as I unpacked all the glass you had given me as it seemed so pretty here and then I sobbed as I read the inscriptions in your books! There are still lots of people to see, though, which keeps me from morose brooding. The first snowy night I spent with Caroline in her cosy Greenwich Village house with the Bacon paintings and baby taking an active part in a babychair next to the fire. I like both her and her husband, Israel Citkovitz. He is very sympathetic with a wry sense of humour. But one feels simply dreadful, headachy from the heating, with a carbohydrate rash. Hamburgers have begun to pall, they're just for the dogs, really. I have been chasing round interviewing people for jobs. Jason E. was amiable and ineffective. Tomorrow I am being interviewed by the editor of the *New Yorker*, Mr Shawn. I am sure I can work it for you to write something, even an article on cartoonists, with all these Christmas potboilers just out. Am going to Gerda's for Christmas. Write to me at her address, as I might do a bunk from this apartment. Heaps of love and let's keep up our peckers . . . B.

Finally, Doubleday's on Fifth Avenue took me on as a temporary saleslady to cope with the Christmas rush. First one had to attend a course of instruction on how to use a cash register, develop a sales technique, 'never assume a customer's potential is exhausted by one sale . . . avoid extremes of dress . . .' The customer had to be greeted pleasantly with the time of day and after a purchase asked if he would care for it to be gift-wrapped. The telephone had to be answered with 'Merry Christmas from Doubleday'. The salary was $45 a week, with a bonus of $10 a week on completion of the six-week sentence. They certainly knew what they were doing! But for a ten-minute break morning and afternoon, and the lunch hour, it meant standing seven hours a day. Each time the head of the department caught one leaning against a pile of books, he'd bark, 'Come along now, none of that.' Women would come in and peruse a cookbook for an hour.
'Can I help you, madam?'

'Just browsing,' was the stock reply.

In the evenings, the buses were crammed with exhausted shoppers slumped over packages. I would join the surge along Fifth Avenue lined with Bowery bums, each one rigged out as Father Christmas, braving the icy wind as he stood swinging a censer to attract shoppers into the big stores. On Madison Avenue, no matter the time of day or the weather, a gaping crowd would be gathered outside one of the big banks, where a bevy of pretty girls with bare arms and bunting-trimmed skirts, each one clasping the next one's shoulder, would be spinning round the main hall on rollerskates. A $60 bonus was not for the likes of me.

Darling Cyril,

Have been suffering from terrible insomnia for ages; I am not unhappy anymore, just worried, mainly about money. Anyway, here is your piece, and I am afraid it's not typed too well . . . 'Count On Me' has gone into the *New Yorker*, but I doubt if they will take it. A friend on their staff, a writer, thought the story was very original and, after helping me correct it, said it had a good chance. I also have a new admirer, a musician, and he conducts – Jewish, of course. So I am not at a loss for company. I see Caroline regularly, and Earl, Old B. and Gerda, and lots of new people, so you see it is better than London; it's just a question of how to earn money in the least obnoxious way. I am sorry you are having a bad time with D. I thought it would get better when I left, but Cressida looks a dream. Otherwise, cannot think of any news; spent New Year in China-town at a marvellous Chinese restaurant. Little pigeons and delicious tender lobster and snow peas. Would like to write a more amusing letter but feel too wreckish. I didn't get any cable at Christmas and was rather hurt, but then realised I hadn't sent you one, after all. I miss you very much at times and get fretful if there is a long gap. Another dull letter. Heaps and heaps of love . . .

February 6 1961
22 W 56th Street
There is a blizzard again; it is supposed to be the worst winter ever. The temperature gets below zero at times. Thick snow, with doormen shovelling and people picking their way along car ruts. I have now moved into a good room. Big, with a usable open fire where one burns some stuff called 'Canel' that blazes up like petroleum; and there is quite a stretch of sky – 'That little patch of blue that prisoners call the sky'. Charlie arranged it for me; it belongs to Maeve Brenan, a friend of his. I sent your piece to Brendan Gill, who is a writer for the *New Yorker*. He is an admirer of yours; if it comes

back I will try *Partisan*. The change of title a great improvement, it made me laugh a lot, the *Believing*. Dwight Macdonald had a piece refused by the *Sat Eve Post* and had to resort to *Partisan*. 'Count on Me' was returned. The man who read it said the homosexual theme would keep it out of everything. But when one sees the competent boredom that goes into the *New Yorker*, one really despairs.

I have no job, at the moment, although am supposed to be working part time for this research company. They don't give me enough work, but they want to keep me on because of the English voice. What one's sunk to. Everybody raves about Kennedy. Have not done anything amusing, been busy getting settled in.

The cold is atrocious. Sacha Schneider has gone off on a tour of the States for two months. Another egomaniac, middle-aged baby.'

Married three times, the last wife being the actress Geraldine Page, Sacha was known as a 'violinist-conductor-impresario-straordinario'.

'Homogeneity is the vorst thing in music,' he would say. 'It is not so good in marriage, either. The first five bars sound vonderful, but aftervards you are bored because everything sounds the same.'

He prided himself on being a great womaniser and lived downtown in a large duplex loft, dominated by a Steinway. Small and energetic, with a leonine head, he would rush round in a dressing gown, a tassel swinging in his wake, preparing delicious meals. He loved food. He had achieved fame as a member of the Budapest String Quartet, the best-known ensemble in the States since 1938 when he arrived with his cellist brother, both of them refugees from Europe. They became a household name; there had even been a cartoon showing four men with masks coming out of a bank holding violin cases and the caption read, 'Let them go, fellas, they're the Budapest Quartet.' But after so many years *ensemble*, they became slipshod and often played out of tune. In 1961, the Quartet was disbanded. Sacha was a generous man. Once, before flying off with his violin to San Francisco, he handed me some dollars that I promptly left behind in a taxi. He entrusted me with the keys to his duplex so that I could come and go as I pleased. Each summer he spent in the Vaucluse where he had a house on the edge of the village of Roussillon.

Darling Cyril,

Thank you very much for your letter. Everything is alright again now, touch wood. Have got a job with Caroline's dentist. He's a capper. I stand in a nurse's uniform getting spattered with blood, holding the patients' hands while their teeth get filed down to vicious little spikes. It's known as 'rehabilitation'. Then the whole lot get gleaming caps. He's threatened to have a look at my mouth, which I'm dreading. I'm going through the whole works . . . swabbing out mouths, aiming the water squirt on the needle as he manipulates the drill, sterilising the burrs, dabbing the patients' chins and administering shots of Bourbon to everyone at the end of the day.

Chuck has lent me his apartment for the whole of the summer. It's got a TV and a record player, friendly cockroaches and a fridge stuffed with frankfurters and pineapple juice. I adore Chuck. He's less treacherous than Earl, has more sentimentality and a gentler disposition. Chuck, Caroline, Israel and the dentist are my favourite people, at the moment. Yesterday, it was sweltering. One had to shed every particle of clothing and even lying motionless on the bed, one sweated. Have gone off the boil for letter writing . . . I'm going to stand on my own feet from now on, providing they don't drop off . . .

The next job was modelling in the Junior Miss department of Bergdorf Goodman's. There were twenty salesladies in the department, their ages ranging from forty to sixty; all had varicose veins and were determined to be friendly. Each time I caught the eye of one of them she'd smile. It became quite a strain. A rictus smile on my face, I'd lean furtively against the glass counter of the Better Hats – little skullcaps dotted with velvet ribbons and bows – and wait for the hostess to take a coffee break, then I'd volunteer for her chair. The hostess sat in the centre of the department answering questions like, 'Do you have anything in toast or pumpkin for my wife?' I would call over one of the smiling hostesses. It gave me something to do, memorising their names. Sometimes, nodding towards a woman wearing drainpipe trousers and an old raincoat, one of them would point out a celebrity.

'There's Katharine Hepburn! Isn't she just darling?'

One never got a smile out of Miss Eric, the head of the department.

'Now watch your step,' she would say, every time she passed and saw my legs comfortably screwed corkscrew fashion under the hostess chair. 'Watch how Doris does it. She's more refined.' Or, 'Look at your hair. I've never seen anything like it. Go to the beauty saloon and get it teased. How often do I have to remind you to put on pancake?' I'd wait for Miss Eric to go to luncheon and then sneak into the airless, cramped model room. But immediately a head would appear round the door and say, 'Have you coasted yet today, dear?' Dressed in one of the latest models, a hat dangling with price labels, I'd get into the lift and tour the other floors, lingering in the antique department, as it never had any customers. The last straw was when Caroline came in pretending to look for a bargain on one of the rails and I was ordered to twirl.

I went from job to job. When out of work I lived on Social Security and a weekly cheque would arrive in the post. Sometimes, I lined up with the rest of the jobless in an Employment Exchange and filled in a resumé which had to be clear, brief and factual:

Be objective. But don't hesitate to present yourself in the best possible light. Give name, height and education. This presented a problem, for I couldn't really claim to have had any.

The only job I really enjoyed was secretary to Joseph Dever, the ginger-haired society editor of the *New York World Telegram* (a daily that soon after became defunct). In order to be close to their office, I moved downtown and took a room overlooking Puerto Ricans in the Chelsea Hotel. I was the only woman in a roomful of about sixty men, 90 of them Jewish. I did not have to clock in to work before ten o'clock. I was in my element. Occasionally, Jo took me to a charity dinner or dance, or I would be included in a group of senators and their wives at a reserved table in the Peppermint Lounge, where café society adults now 'dug Juves New Beat' and everyone was 'Doin' the Twist' to Joey Dee and his Starliters. Cholly Knickerbocker* claimed to have discovered the Peppermint Lounge and, writing under 'American Smart Set', put:

I wandered into a Broadway honky-tonk to find the place filled with sailors, GIs, young folk in sweaters and tight pants, gyrating – the eternally young Col Serge Obolensky joined in the fray. The next day I wrote it up and it is now the hottest place in town. The dancers scarcely touch or move their feet. Everything else, however, moves. The upper body sways forward and backward and the hips and shoulders twirl erotically while the arms thrust out up and down with the piston-like motions of a baffled bird-keeper fighting off a flock of attacking blue jays . . .

Though a solidly built fellow, Bob Silvers was a topping twister. He counselled me to imagine I had just stepped out of a bath and was briskly towelling my buttocks, but one only had to be seen motionless on the crowded dancefloor to get a reputation of 'livin' it up'. My main task on the 'Society' column was to take down particulars of forth-coming deb marriages over the telephone (an instrument I generally shun), confining conversation to the minimum. There was such a jabber going on in the crowded room I often lost track of an essential detail. Anxiety led to inaudibility. I couldn't hear what anybody was saying. One day, because of this, I omitted to pass on a message to Jo from his broker, advising him to sell some stocks quickly. Jo never forgave me, even after I had humiliated myself by begging to be kept on in the job. Instead, he rendered me totally ridiculous by writing an over-laudatory reference:

As my alter-ego it was Miss Skelton's considerable task to edit all copy, develop story material, supervise the special *débutante* issue, show the flag

---

* Pseudonym of Hearst-syndicated gossip columnist.

at myriad charity affairs, all of which she accomplished with ease, imagination and flair. She has had a varied spectrum of experience, ranging from wartime code clerk to Cordon-Bleu cooking. Her first book won the immediate respect of the London literary coterie, of which she is still a member in good standing . . .

This led to no further employment.

Though strictly out of bounds to Americans since the Bay of Pigs, I planned a trip to Cuba. Gerda had moved to Washington where her husband had become aide to Senator Dodge. While applying for a visa from the US Department of Justice, I went to stay with her in Centreville where one day a letter arrived: 'Permission to depart for Cuba from the United States is not authorised. Sincerely, Supervisory Immigrant Inspector.' So I decided to fly in from Jamaica.

Chapter XIII

Cuba

'Don't expect to eat much where you're going,' said the girl in the Kingston KLM office, as she filled in a return ticket to Havana. After eating a quick lunch of curried goat, I rushed to the airport to find the runway swarming with British officials armed with swords, awaiting the arrival of the Duke of Edinburgh. I boarded the plane feeling like a criminal. Then, to the ominous words, 'We'd like to say goodbye to our disembarking passengers,' two Germans, a French diplomat and myself stepped on to Jose Martin runway as, with frightened, averted eyes, a Cuban family hurried past to occupy our vacant seats. The customs check was courteous and thorough. Any dollars had to be handed over and changed into pesos, jewellery declared and its value assessed. Fleeing Cubans were not allowed to take out any money or jewellery, and were limited to two pairs of shoes and two dresses. Where was I going to stay? The Inglaterra.

'We'd prefer you to stay in the Hotel Colina,' said the ground hostess.

The Hotel Colina was dingy. There was no soap and the basin had no stopper. A previous visitor's cigarette stub lay under the bed. It was drizzling and there was a strong north wind. I asked the way to the sea. it was bashing the wall that bordered the waterfront and spray spattered the pavement. Every few blocks a militia man dozed over a rifle. On the corner of the main shopping street was a billboard with the message 'Construct and Defend our Socialist Fatherland'. Posted outside a large office building were a group of militia girls in short-sleeved, sky-blue shirts, khaki trousers and boots, each one taking a turn to comb her hair before a mirror propped on a rifle butt.

That evening, for an hour, I walked in search of a bar. Should it be the Club La Red or the Tokao? Descending some steps I entered a dimly lit cavern. To enliven the place, the barman put on a rumba. Cuban Coca Cola accompanied the Bacardi I ordered. At the bar I tried to read. No candles? A nightlight was produced. The waiters were curious to see what I was reading. They inspected the KLM matches, as Cuban matches did not strike. There was usually a band in the evening, they said, but the permanent staff were off. They have a holiday on Mondays.

'For the *Revolución*,' someone said and giggled, as if he had made a subversive joke.

'Is it considered bad for women to come to bars alone?' I asked.

'Oh no. They like to dance,' said a man seated on the adjoining stool. 'Here it's alright' – meaning at the bar – 'but not in there.' He pointed to a dungeoned alcove. He said he was a doctor and worked at the university hospital. He'd learnt English at school. His manner was gentle, he was very tall and, as far as one could see, had several teeth missing. His fifteen-year-old son was in America. His brother, a dentist, had also left Cuba. He disapproved of doctors and dentists leaving; they should stay and care for the people. 'The barman is saying you are a Czech. We haven't seen any English for two years . . .'

We took a taxi and went to several downtown bars. In one we asked if there was anything to eat.

'I'd like to come to your tourist hotel and get a good meal,' said the barman.

We walked around the harbour for an hour. Above a wharf, opposite the Spanish Embassy, was a large drawing of a donkey and written across it was the word 'KENNEDY'. Underneath it said, 'All the world is being educated but me, and you can see what I am, a DONKEY.'

There were billboards everywhere with the word '*FISMINUTOS*', and Léger-like figures were depicted with rolled-up sleeves as if about to perform gymnastics, and the injunction, '¡*REVOLUCIONARIOS!* Increase Production, Eliminate Absenteeism and Help the Country'.

'And look at them,' the doctor jeered, pointing to the militiamen posted every few years, 'mostly old Batistianos.' Suddenly he stopped. 'Hi there!' he said, and gave a dozing old guard a playful prod with his rifle. 'He's a friend of mine.' They greeted each other affectionately. 'Old rogue,' he bantered, and the guard laughed. 'He's against the government, aren't you? And there he is working for them.' The doctor said his friend had been imprisoned during Batista's time. He had fought for Castro. 'But look at him now.' We passed another poster. He mimicked the pointing finger. 'And look what we have for entertainment': *Fatherland or Death* was showing at the movie house. We crossed some gardens shaded by giant coconut palms. 'This is called Central Park, because it's the centre of the city.' He laughed. 'But it's beautiful.'

'Certainly it's beautiful,' I echoed. He pointed to the old limestone buildings festooned with 'Long Live the International Proletariat' and the impressive white Capitol dominating the downtown section, now embellished with *Fatherland or Death*.

It was one in the morning. He thought he knew of a place to eat, the other side of the park. We entered an open bar with a horseshoe-shaped counter, around which men and prostitutes sat and joked about food.

'What would you like? Macaroni? Dry rice or potatoes?' One man crouched over his plate of macaroni, jovially raised his fork and shouted something in Spanish, before filling his mouth with the gluey mixture. Everybody laughed. 'He said he's imagining it's ham.' The doctor found me a taxi, patted my cheek as he said 'Goodnight' and vanished through Central Park. At the door of the Hotel Colina the taximan asked if I like to dance, as he knew of a very good rumba club.

For breakfast there was orange juice, chunks of guava jelly and excellent *espresso* coffee. The hotel was full, from families on their way out to the country, who attended meals with shopping bags, to militia girls and students. I took a bus to the British Embassy. The ticket had a little figure of an alarm clock with a face on spindly legs and underneath: 'Down with Absenteeism. Worker ... Arrive punctually at your job, because that is the way we will construct Socialism.'

Cubans then had charming manners. I never had to stand on a bus. And they took a lot of trouble when showing the way, silently walking you to your destination and depositing you right on the doorstep. To attract attention, whether hailing a friend or a waiter, they would go 'pisst', lingering on the hiss with an abrupt end on the 't' sound. The Embassy was a solid haven of out-of-date newspapers. They said it was not necessary to report there, but advised me to go immediately to the immigration bureau for permission to leave the country, otherwise my departure might be held up for weeks.

Walking around Havana remained a continuous source of pleasure, with the streets lined with ceiba trees, and everywhere squares and gardens were filled with exotic plants. At one of the bookstalls in the Paseo del Prado, amongst the paperbacks by Marx and Lenin, and *The Diary of Anne Frank*, I found a 1953 guide. Sitting in Central Park, I read that *'cuba'* means jar of oil and that Cuba is the only West Indian island to retain its name; that Columbus loved every island he saw, calling each one beautiful, but Cuba was the most beautiful that eyes have ever seen; and that Havana, founded in 1519, had the oldest university of the Latin-American countries.

On Avenida de las Misiones, a fresh shipload of tractors gleamed in the sun, parked in regimental files around the statue of General Gomez. Students with armfuls of books poured in and out of the Havana Libre, which used to be the Hilton. The hotel restaurant had become a canteen serving macaroni, rice and potato, with an occasional blob of fish. The dessert was always the same — guava jelly or sweetened coconut purée. On the twenty-fifth floor, the highest point in the city, Congress groups surged in and out of the Havana Libre bar, or conversed in whispers.

'An American,' one member said, nudging her companion and pointing at me, as if the wonders of Havana would never cease.

At Floridati, the photographs of Hemingway had been removed from the bar and the restaurant was empty. There were no Morro crabs, no menu.

'Fishermen don't go out as they used,' said the waiter, 'and when they do, they have to be accompanied by an armed guard.'

Albert came into the bar. He was eighteen, very tall, pale and spotty. He spoke a little American. He had come to lend a hand with the drums, as the regular drummer was ill. His father was in Miami and his younger brother in Ohio. He lived with his mother, who worked in a restaurant. Why didn't he get a regular job? He wanted to be a drummer. He couldn't get a job in a band, as he lacked cymbals and you couldn't find them in Cuba any more. Why did he carry a lucky charm? Someone had given it him when he came out of prison. Four years previously he had been one of Castro's guerrillas and had planted home-made bombs in factories at night. Now he got odd jobs cleaning cars. He was a kind of dead-end kid. He liked smoking thirty-five-cent cigars, said he had $1,000 in the bank, but there was nothing he could buy with it.

'Supposing you wanted to buy a new car?'

'The new cars go to the government.'

He was going on to a jazz club. Did I like jazz? His friend Amando had just started a club. We ran into Amando, who was very handsome, with a small blonde beard and gentle manner.

'It's very existentialist,' he said, 'just a converted old movie studio. There are four of us: sax, piano, bass and drums.'

The jazz club was like a stalactite cavern, with dim lighting and midnight-blue walls, and a high, arched ceiling. Bearded militiamen sat with their arms round coloured girls who had peaked-wig hairsets, straight cotton dresses and patent-leather shoes.

'The trouble is, people won't come here; being jazz, they think it's American. Man, I'm hungry.' The waiter brought Bacardis and a dish with one boiled egg. The three of us shared the egg. Amando asked for another. But the waiter said there weren't any. Amando had been earning good money in the States. He'd only been back four months. Why did he come back? His wife kept writing to say she and the baby were starving. 'I don't get on with my wife, but I love my little girl.' The sax player joined our table. He wore a beret, came from Chicago and was a nutty American communist. He'd been to London.

'What were you doing there?'

'Visiting Marx's tomb, of course. What else?'

Parallel to the coast, beyond the Havana Riviera Hotel, along Fifth Avenue, was the section where, everyone liked to tell you, the millionaires used to live. It stretched for some miles, a beautiful, tree-lined avenue of small palaces that had been turned into student quarters. The Casino nearby had been converted into a school. Along the sandy coast, known as the Concha, the luxury clubs had been turned into public beaches, the gardens were luxuriant with flowering trees, and bordering each drive was a boathouse filled with jacked-up sailing-boats and motor launches with peeling paint, sad emblems of the departed rich. Lying on the sands in the shade of a dwarf coconut tree facing a palatial, white club building, one could focus on a banner with 'Viva Internacionalismo Proletario' strung across the portico. 'With Fidel til Death' was notched into the barks of the palm trees. One swam to the continuous strains of the International.

On Sundays, endless busloads were disgorged at the beaches. The women still seemed uncertain as to how to react to their good fortune and cringed, fully dressed, on the edge of the sea in a state of joyful bewilderment, until the heat drove them into purple celanese bathing costumes. They rarely ventured into the water, but lay giggling on the fringe like basking limpets, while the men flung fistfuls of sand or buried one of their companions and then thrust a stick in beside or on top of him as a phallic symbol. A waiter who used to be a member of one of the luxury clubs said his property had been confiscated and one day I was kept bobbing at the end of a pool for an hour listening to an aristocratic old gentleman telling me about his losses, including his daughters, one of whom had emigrated to Folkestone. He spoke about it gaily. One of their old servants, aged seventy, who had spent her life savings on a small retirement house, had had it taken away and now didn't have enough to live on. That can't be right, he said. But he was going to stay, just to see the regime change. After all, Batista had been bad enough.

A retired naval officer who had lost his pension and home described himself as a pauper and laughed. A pauper, he repeated. I said I was too. But I was used to it. Things will change, he said, everyone was convinced of it. They dreamt of being rescued by the Americans one day.

One night, in the hotel lift, an air-force officer remarked on my cold. He said he had had a cold for days.

'I'm a pilot and fly at very high altitudes, and experience a constant change of temperature.' Whisky had cured him. He had some whisky in his room. Would I like some? I accepted a toothglass and drank it standing in the passage. Suitably enough, it was Cuban whisky and tasted of cough mixture. he said wouldn't I come in? He wanted to show me his Czech machine-gun. See how easy it is to handle, he said. Joking, I asked him not to keep pointing it in my direction. He was very simple and charming, and brought out a copy of Playa Girón, the book about the American invasion. It contained references to himself. 'Here I am, you see, here it refutes all the lies the Americans said about me, that I'm a traitor.' In 1959 he had been smuggling arms into Cuba from Miami. 'We used to store them in a disused theatre, the Rainbow. What's more,' he said, 'I know the exiles are using the same theatre right now, for the same purpose.' He liked the English, he said. What did they think about Cuba? Why are the Americans giving arms to all the Latin-American countries? To invade Cuba?

Over breakfast one morning, a Chilean joined my table; very small with black hair and the excitable manner of a recent arrival, he was wearing tropical army uniform and 'beaten-gold' bracelets, bought in Mexico, whence he had come to seek political asylum. He said he was an underground communist and had an American passport. He seemed to have chosen this moment to leave in order to avoid the clutches of the army. He was aggressive about the Royal Family. Why did England keep it? It was just a question of time ... the world would see ... Would I like to accompany him to the immigration bureau? First he was going to see a friend. The friend was Guatemalan. He had come from America.

'I came here six months ago. I knew no one and felt so miserable that I at once fell sick.' Would I like to visit the Isle of Pines? I said I had arranged to go to Pinar del Rio that day. They were delighted and took me to the bus terminal. 'The *Transportes Populares* is a unit in itself,' the Guatemalan said, 'they have their own stores, dentists and doctors for the staff and their families.' Did I know about the LTP services for the people? 'Well,' he related like someone telling a wondrous tale, 'when the rich people left Cuba, all their cars were taken by the LTP, and all the women who had been working for the rich fifteen hours a day like slaves were put in a school and trained as drivers. We gave them uniforms, the cars were painted red and now anyone can take one of these cars for twenty cents.' Later, someone explained that these taxis follow the same route as the buses, which are always breaking down. And since no more spare parts could be got for American cars, the service would eventually become extinct.

Hairdressers had run out of bobby pins, rollers and hairnets. In order not to deprive them of the satisfaction of using hairspray, which they did still have, I let them tease my hair into a wig. But it was not this, nor the sweetened cigarettes (due to processed sugarcane paper), nor the endless topic of Cuba so much as the monotonous diet of starch that made me glad to leave. There was one good restaurant in Havana, the Miami, with a high ceiling, mirrored walls lined with potted plants, a vase of tuberoses on a white cloth at every table, pale green curtains and chair covers. On one side was a cigar counter and a bar where pineapples and mameys were stacked. I would go there expressly to drink large draughts of fresh pineapple juice with a dash of *citron* and the pastries were delicious.

'After all,' said the waiter, 'we do get flour from Russia,' adding that the mameys were only good for icecream.

Though the return flight was scheduled to depart at 12.25, all passengers other than diplomats had to report to the airport at eight in the morning.

When the luggage had been checked, I ran into a Reuter correspondent. He was awaiting the arrival of prisoners taken hostage during the American invasion. He took me up to the press balcony overlooking the deserted runway. The prisoners were due to arrive from the prison at 9.30. We kept scouring the horizon for some sign of life. In the distance, a Canadian plane took off, having deposited a cargo of meat that got flown into Havana twice a week. When the first car pulled up on the runway, the negotiators stepped out and some time later Castro's car drove up. When the Pan Am plane landed to take the prisoners away, two journalists got out. They were not allowed up into the press room, so they stood on the runway shouting up at fellow reporters. Jokes were made to the effect that the delay must be caused by Kennedy's cheque having bounced. A French reporter shouted down that he was no longer allowed to telephone. Another kept shouting down scraps of information. The prisoners had been well treated . . . there was still a small colony of Americans in Havana, living quietly and unmolested.

'I hope you don't get into trouble,' someone said to me, 'but you should have reported to the snakepit downstairs an hour ago.' A few days back a woman journalist had been searched and had missed her plane for having a stack of hotel notepaper in her suitcase; it was thought that she had made notes in invisible ink. I remained long enough to see two buses draw alongside the Pan Am plane, and the sick and wounded, wearing odd trousers and shirts, some with missing limbs, sadly and silently boarded the plane which took off immediately. The vacated runway instilled a sense of desolation. There was chaos down in the lobby. It took an hour for everyone's papers to be scrutinised. Cubans were having to exhibit their valueless baubles. One decrepit old Negress said, 'I've got to leave, I'm sick, you see.' Men's breast pockets were stuffed with cigars but their suitcases were practically empty.

I had thoroughly enjoyed my visit. The Cubans I had met had struck me as being very gentle, humorous and friendly. But it was a relief to get back to Kingston and see Jamaicans in flowered hats contentedly trooping off to church as a fashion show was being held round the hotel swimming pool.

Then I boarded a cruise ship. On arrival in Miami I left my passport stamped with a Cuban visa in the care of the cruise ship's Greek purser and entered the United States with an immigration card.

Back in New York, I stayed in the Hotel Fourteen, or in Charlie's little house on Long Island. He was then passionately attached to Joan Fontaine. Though still pretty, the actress had become rather stout and most exacting, it was said. I came upon them at a party given by the journalist, Gavin Young, who always invited people from various *milieux* and gave large, amusing parties in New York. Some wondered how he managed it on *Observer* pay. Intending to be friendly, I went up to Joan Fontaine. I cannot remember what I said, but she immediately took offence and flounced out, leaving Charlie at the party.

Though known to be incapable of retaining the simplest employment, the incident increased my popularity, for it looked as though I had scored over this glamorous lady. Even Gavin, whom I wrongly assumed to be a misogynist, seemed impressed and embraced me with abandon on his doorstep when I left – a gesture, alas, that was never repeated. But eventually we became good friends.

Bob then took me to live with him in a large airy apartment over Carnegie Hall that the pianist, Peter Duchin, had lent him for the summer. Not that I saw much of Bob. He spent nights on 33rd Street rewriting articles for *Harper's*. He would turn up for breakfast with 'Hello, Kiddo' and slip into the bed as I was stepping out. Infinitely more sympathetic and kinder, but with less energy (in order to keep going he took stimulants that he handed on to me) and a slogger in more ways than one, Bob struck me as being very similar to Weidenfeld. Determined to lure Bob into his publishing firm, W. surfaced again at this point, saying to Bob, 'Don't think for a moment that I minimise the difficulties that you would face in making the major change of leaving *Harper's* and coming to work for us . . . as to financial terms I of course sympathise with your point of view looking at figures from an American angle.' In spite of W.'s persistence when he was out to get what he wanted – 'Perhaps we can collaborate all the same by your acting as an adviser . . .' – Bob remained uninterested. It was only after a lengthy newspaper strike that Bob left *Harper's* to become an editor on the newly founded *New York Review of Books*.

As to W., he faded out altogether until over twenty years later when, to my surprise, he rang me up from London. I was living in Seine-et-Marne.

'Your voice hasn't changed at all,' he said. 'I hear you're writing an auto-biography.'

To reassure him, I replied, 'Yes. But I haven't got on to you yet.'

'I'm in the throes of writing mine,' he confided, 'and I've said some very nice things about you.' The conversation was brief and terminated by him saying, 'As you live in the country I expect you'd like me to send you some books.' My voice might not have changed. Neither had his character. It was about this time that he was aligning himself with Getty and opening up a branch of his publishing house in New York.

No books arrived. So I wrote a rather snappy note saying 'How typical!' A month later, two parcels arrived simultaneously. The books had been sent in duplicate and included two art books and two copies of A. J. Ayer's *Wittgenstein*, together with two copies of a first novel by Paul Pickering, *Wild About Harry* – none of them, alas, readable. Since then, Taki has written in *The Spectator* that he ran into Weidenfeld in Italy where 'our noble lord, since receiving a knighthood at the same time as the Beatles' honour, has been staying at a house taken by two rich and ageing but very elegant American ladies. No sooner had he arrived than a native reported he had seen an escaped baboon and the fuzz arrived. Upon closer inspection of the property, the "baboon" turned out to be nothing more lethal than our George, sunning himself in the nude. Apparently, this noble lord's secret charm – published here for the first time – is that he is covered with hair from head to foot, including his buttocks.' Weidenfeld is quoted as saying that Taki would never have been able to get away with what he does if it weren't for the protection he gets from four people: Gianni Agnelli, David Somerset, Tony Lambton and John Aspinall.

'But I do understand why the great publisher feels the way he does. After all, protection comes to him naturally. He married one of America's richest, La Payson, and now is friendly with an even richer one, La Getty. Protection is his middle name . . .'

After Taki wrote this, inquisitive people kept ringing me to check on W.'s buttocks.

Whether it was tit-for-tat or merely incidental, Joan Fontaine vamped Bob's-your-uncle and afterwards Charlie told me she had found it very heavy going. By then I had moved into an apartment on East 83rd, delegated by Earl, who had upgraded to the fifties. Known as a railroad apartment that you entered through the kitchen, with a sitting room on one side and a slit of a bedroom on the other, it was quiet and had a view of the sky. Opposite was a wasteland. In fine weather, one could climb on to the roof and sunbathe in a deckchair. The rent was $75 a month. Although I always referred to the building as a slum, I was very happy living there throughout the next two years. Those prepared to mount five dun flights smelling of cats and cabbage were pleasantly surprised on entering to see a Sidney Nolan, 'Bird Over Harbour', and some pretty English furniture.

A piece on Cuba came out in *The London Magazine* and was picked up by an American monthly, *Atlas*, under the title, 'In the Streets of Havana'. *Atlas*, the magazine of the World Press, dealt only in current affairs in translations and reprints from abroad. This resulted in a fan letter from Mr Morrow, a West Coast publisher, friend of the poet Kenneth Rexroth, whom I had met in San Francisco. Morrow Books specialised in mysticism and religion. Alan Ross went on encouraging me to write. Like someone ordering a baker's dozen, he sent postcards saying, 'Another short story, please. How many does that add up to now? I think your last is one of your very best, though perhaps the last line is a bit flat.' Whereupon, I would sit down and mint out another one. When Morrow came to offer me a job as his secretary, I was bent over the typewriter and looked so ashen that before committing himself he insisted on my having a check-up with his doctor. At that time, future employers demanded a certificate of health, exonerating you from any venereal disease, as nowadays it might be AIDS. Then Morrow took me to meet his wife. The Morrows lived out of New York on a turnpike, where they eventually found me a dismal bedsit. Morrow had a tiny office. His room was next to mine. From where I sat, with earphones attached to my head, I could see him through a glass pane and when not questioning his spelling (as we know American and English words do not always tally) I typed to his dictation. To my horror, in less than a month, I once more became deaf. I could see his lips moving, but could not decipher a word. Morrow lost no time, which is probably why he now has a flourishing publishing house. He dismissed me kindly, recommending his analyst.

Soon after, I received the following: 'Dear Barbara, You are a very wonderful person and you should learn to respect yourself as much as those who love you do. The name of my psychiatrist is Dr Grace Baker 214 E. 61st.' It was signed 'the Rev Dr McKelway', a manic-depressive writer on the *New Yorker*.

It was Caroline's psychiatrist who got me in the end. What attracted me was that he analysed with the aid of LSD. He was lanky, like my father, and had a small brush moustache. I had no trouble in getting a transference, which is supposed to be so important, once you go in for that sort of thing. The first session, Longman (I think he was named) questioned me about my childhood relationship with Daddy.

'For something got fouled up somewhere along the line and we've got to set you up so that you can fend for yourself.'

'Daddy used to take me for walks,' I confessed, 'but we never had any conversation.' From then on, when I entered his room, Longman merely handed me a glass of water and the LSD pills, and sat waiting for a latent repression to surface (what is known as an 'abreaction' – resolution of a neurosis by reviving repressed or forgotten ideas of an event). The night after the first session, I dreamt of Daddy covered in blood rushing to attack me. Each session lasted four hours, during which I lay on the couch occasionally seeing goblins or breasts that turned into roses; but apart from that, nothing much. LSD affects the vision. The most ordinary object, like a necktie, can take on peculiar patterns and vivid colouring, and paintings appear magical. 'You've got to get right in there,' Longman kept saying each time he increased the dose. He got so little out of me that he would put on a Tchaikovsky symphony and leave the room. At the end of each session, with blazing eyes, I would be helped like an invalid into a taxi by his assistant-mistress, who was a reformed drug addict. Once she was out of sight, I dismissed the taxi and strode euphorically downtown to Caroline's, and we sat up half the night ridiculing Longman and comparing our reactions. Longman was very indiscreet. In between sessions, he seemed to enjoy revealing the idiosyncrasies of other patients, one of whom, apparently, hoarded excreta in the rectum for weeks. It was due to him, Longman boasted, that Cary Grant had turned to heterosexuality and fathered a child. Once he got on to the fact I was paranoid, on arrival I would be put at the end of the queue and when my turn came,

Longman poked his head round the door and said, as though referring to a female Tom Thumb, 'Has anyone seen Miss Skelton today?' All it did was to paralyse me with inferiority. Then, one day, after a session, I went straight on to a party. When I entered the room all the men appeared to have long flowing beards. In the taxi going home, I looked into the windscreen mirror and glimpsed Mummy as a toad. Longman merely whistled when I told him. But I could see he was excited. At last we seemed to be getting somewhere. The session over, he asked for money. When I said I didn't have any, that was that. Psychiatrists claim that if they are not paid, analysis will never do a patient any good. All the experience taught me was that depression is due to the repression of an impulse and that a penchant for corpulent men implied a subconscious desire to abnegate poor Daddy, who had been as slim as a rake.

Chapter XIV

Aftermath

A block away on 83rd Street, James Lord lived with a young man who was training to be a singer. Larry never attained his ambition: some said that he was incapable of memorising a libretto. James had written a very good short story called *The Boy Who Wrote No*, which had come out in *Horizon* and I was thrilled to have him as a neighbour. Since then, after twenty years' research, he has published a biography of the sculptor Giacometti, whom he knew and admired. I saw a lot of Jim in New York and whenever I went round to his apartment, Larry's voice would be reverberating along the corridor. Jim was very kind in those days. There was a carpenter in our street where we bought the planks, and Jim made some bookshelves and hammered them on to the wall behind my bed. A perfectionist in matters of taste, he invested in modern paintings and precious objects. The armchairs and sofa in his spacious apartment were covered in muted blue, nothing was out of place and the paintings had been hung with precisely the right amount of space in between. His Paris apartment now resembles a small museum and not everyone is privileged enough to be allowed in.

To see him unwrapping his valuables was like watching an avid stork brooding over a precious new-born hatch. Jim had some odd foibles. Nothing would induce him to take a taxi. I had another 'standing' job at the time, lifting urns in a tropical plant shop, which did not deter him from insisting on a long walk to the cinema in the evening. The only time I knew him to give a small party, he invited (although he hardly knew them) Caroline and Bob's-your-uncle who were then 'going together'. I can only assume it was to see my reaction. Caroline and I were no longer friends for, from being a delightful companion, she had begun to turn into an angry lady wielding a ferocious pen.

It was about this time that a concerted effort was made on the part of various people to help me obtain a grant from the Ingram Merrill Foundation. Alan Ross wrote to a Mr Ford to say:

Miss Skelton has asked me to sponsor her for a grant. I have published several short stories by her and hope to do a book of them early next year. I consider her someone of original and remarkable talent, who if she had the means to devote herself freely to writing, would greatly reward the investor . . .

Stephen wrote:

She is a most talented and serious writer and I think that she would make good use of a grant and do some very good stories or a novel . . .

Alan Pryce-Jones wrote to say he was glad to be a sponsor:

I have known her for a good many years – since she was first married to Cyril Connolly, an old friend of forty years, and then to George Weidenfeld, also someone I have been in touch with since 1945. Miss Skelton is an interesting woman in her own right and has written some excellent pieces. Neither of her former husbands give her more than a pittance . . . and I know her circumstances are painfully restricted. She has a real small talent and if any assistance can be given her, she would, I know, carry through any project she may have in mind to a successful conclusion . . .

Nothing came of it. Then Jean Liedloff did her bit:

To Whom It May Concern . . . I have known Miss Barbara Skelton for four years and have found her to be of the highest character, very fond of children and an excellent housekeeper. I can highly recommend her as a babysitter; she is extremely orderly and a very good cook, having graduated from the Cordon Blue [sic] School of Cooking in London with honours.

And so it was that I spent the most depressing Christmas of my life babysitting. Doan wrote: 'Meilleurs voeux pour 1963. Vous me dites rien de votre vie Americaine et me laissez d'imaginer le pire. A mon frère. Il a fait une magnifique exposition de peintures, qui a pour thème la ville rouge et les hommes bleus. Une visiteuse célèbre, Barbara Hutton, est venue. Elle a été séduite par les tableaux et par leur auteur. Ils sont fiancés. Il a quitté son travail de laboratoire et le voici maintenant dans le tourbillon de la vie mondaine et cosmopolite. Actuellement, il est au Mexique où Barbara possède une villa paradisiaque. Et *vous chère autre Barbara, donnez-moi de vos nouvelles. Affection, Thai . . .'* At this stage of his life, Doan, who had a French father and Chinese mother, seemed to have opted for the more exotic side of his parentage.

I had met Jean at a party given by the Rolos, when she was a striking James Bond Viking, and we immediately became friends. Financed by several rich optimists, she had glamorised herself by making two expeditions with a photographer to the Amazon in search of gold. But apart from a thorough knowledge of the piranha fish, a radio broadcast and an article in a magazine, with photos of Jean semi-nude paddling a canoe with a native, nothing came of either expedition. She then got a job writing blurbs for an advertising agency and moved to a sunny apartment with a terrace, in the Sixties. We shared a love of exotic pets. Jean was partial to woolly monkeys. But like all bizarre pets, they lost their lives in tragic circumstances, for they do not mell with urban lives. She acquired her last woolly monkey when it was a baby. Every time I went round to see her, the wretched animal would either be in its cage making clucking noises or squatting beside the fridge frenziedly trying to wrench it open.

'If there's one thing I know about, it's monkeys,' was Jean's stock response. 'You must never give them too much to eat. My mother's instinct tells me it's had enough.'

Two years later, when I was about to leave New York for good, a plump Jean came to see me with her current gentleman friend and the tiny monkey-child, by then fully grown, with rickety legs, totally deformed due to malnutrition, which left the sickening impression that instead of depriving her monkey, Jean should have applied the starvation dictum to herself.

In between babysitting and hauling old ladies out of baths, I went to parties. One invitation went: 'I'll be giving a large and crowded party. Do you think you would like to come? It's from nine o'clock at Central Park West penthouse. Luciana.' I had never met this Italian lady, though I had seen her at other social occasions looking as though her face had been dipped in flour. Her husband was a correspondent for *La Stampa*. The last party I had been to on the West Side had been in the Dakota Building. I shall always remember the occasion as Susan Sontag was accompanied by a very odd girl, and as she, Sontag, Bob and others were leaving the party, she rushed up to everyone, holding out a small black casket, saying. 'Would you like to see what I've got?' Everyone shook her off but me; so she grabbed my arm and flicked open the box, which contained a rotted foetus.

It was at Luciana's party that I met Hamish Hamilton's son who was, in fact, courting the hostess. Alastair maintained we had met already at his parents' house ten years before,* when Cyril and I had been to a dinner party and his

---

* See *Tears Before Bedtime*, Chapter XIV.

mother, Yvonne, had taken me up to her son's cot to bid him goodnight. He had turned into an elegant young man with immense charm. He loved music and then seemed to have a literary bent. And so began one of the most foolhardy affairs of my life that continued briefly on our return to London. With Alastair, my jealousy knew no bounds. He only had to glance at a passing girl in the street for me to sulk. He was then suffering from a kidney complaint and kept flying back to London for medical consultations, and would write describing the gruesome sessions with doctors. His mother, he said, was once more showing him off to her friends, including W. But he was determined to get back to his Darling Little Pussycat. When he did, we lived together in the slum to which he had a spare key. Once he went off on some mysterious weekend to the country and came back unexpectedly to be confronted by Charles Addams. For some inexplicable reason – for he had never done so before – Charlie had spent the night in my apartment and Alastair had let himself in the door as Charlie was scurrying naked into the shower. Whereupon there were fisticuffs with Addams, oddly enough, the victor. As Hamish Hamilton was Charles Addams' London publisher, Alastair rose unabashed to his feet and said, very seriously, 'How do you like the colour process my father has just done on your book?'

Passing through New York in 1982, I went to dine with Charlie on his birthday. Dangling from the ceiling in the sitting room of his apartment was an enormous red balloon sent by the *New Yorker* congratulating him on being seventy. Looking up at it, Charlie kept saying, 'Seventy! But that's aulde, isn't it?' I saw him last in 1986, when he claimed to have given up drinking. He died sadly enough two years later.

The apartment rented to a Brooklyn couple, Alastair and I then took a Greyhound bus heading toward the Mexican border. 'It's such a comfort to Take the Bus. Plan your Trip of a Lifetime. Travel 3,000, 5,000, even 8,000 miles.' I had already done this trip; the ticket then cost $99 and lasted three months. Ceaselessly on the move air-conditioned buses drew in and out of terminals on schedule, and when one arrived in a town, a reliable and courteous albino, with a seared face and neck, would be standing at the base of the coach with a helping hand, saying, with impersonal affability, before trotting happily off duty. 'It's certainly been a pleasure having you folks aboard. I hope you have a pleasant journey.'

I did it during a Christmas rush when hundreds of heated buses were manoeuvring servicemen across country on leave and trusting owl-faced. grey-haired old ladies, wearing plastic-petalled skullcaps, their chests gleaming with silvered mistletoe and holly sprigs, sat dozing about the rest rooms. The buses were comfortable and clean. When not spending the night in a women's hostel, I stretched out at the back of the bus and slept. Seen off by Jane, I left New York for Chicago and from the Dakotas proceeded on to San Francisco.

Travelling through the beautiful state of Montana, an old cowboy took the adjoining seat. When he knew where I came from he asked how we got about in England – on bicycles?

'You like Mexico? Where did you go? By plane direct from a cold climate to the Peurta Vallarta? Or did you fly direct to Yucatan, squat in the Hotel Merida, described as "hot dog" in the Mexican guide, and survey the ruins from a hired car? Are you fastidious? Do you mind what you eat?'

Alastair and I bussed round Mexico. With my basket over his arm, trotting round the Maya ruins where we saw iguanas running about the temples, Alastair became the blue-eyed *burro*.

It was in Mexico City that I attended my final bullfight. Cesar Herón was the matador of the day. As the band struck up he walked into the arena accompanied by a man carrying a ten-year-old boy across his arms. A megaphone explained that the boy was blind. Herón was donating all the proceeds of the afternoon's takings to the hospital to cover the operation for the boy to regain his sight. Would these *aficionados* present like to contribute something for this poor boy who remained stretched out awkwardly in his father's arms? Centivos rained into the arena. As Herón's *equipe* dashed across the sand to gather up the shower of coins, the megaphone claimed, 'We have now reached the sum of . . . generous people . . . we have now reached a further sum of . . .' Then two excessively well-padded picadors entered the arena looking as though they were about to topple over. They were greeted with howls of derision and, from the top tier, cans and bottles literally rained down on their heads. The picadors exited ducking Coca Cola bottles. It had not deterred them from widening the gory gash at the back of the bull's neck.

Six bulls were killed as rapidly and hygienically as possible. Herón was awarded three ears and one departed with the impression of having visited a well-run *abattoir*.

From Vera Cruz Alastair and I flew back to England.

Old friends were scattered. Those I saw greeted me with enigmatic smiles and the refrain, 'Whatever are you going to do now, Barbara?' Old B. was going through yet another divorce. He had written to say he could put me up in his London flat. But when I arrived, finding me, in his words, 'still youthful and attractive to the eye', he tried to tuck me up in his double bed. A rehash with an old lover – I was not that desperate. Then Julian Jebb went abroad and lent me his flat in Maida Vale. Alastair had been packed off to Rome. Ruth Sheradski had just opened an antique shop off Sloane Square. While Ruth scoured other antique shops buying tasteful objects to resell at a profit, she gave me £12 a week to take charge of 'loot'.

But very few people came into the shop and as London remained enveloped in fog, I was soon pining after my Beautyrest bed, early morning exercises with Jack Lalanne on the TV, the amusing people who used to mount my dun stairway and all the art galleries I frequented in New York. So I rang Anne Moynihan who was in the Bouches-du-Rhône and she offered to lend me her large studio-apartment in the rue de Payenne. I flew to Le Bourget. The Spanish maid spoke no English. While rain pattered on the roof for days, I would stand before the window watching little birds hop about a tiny *place* dominated by a catalpa tree. The only person I knew in Paris was an American lady Eileen Geist, who would include me with the children when obliged to take them to an afternoon movie. Otherwise, should I wander round her flat in the rue du Bac, Eileen would be engrossed in doing the editorial work which enabled her to go on filling her wardrobe with high-necked, beaded cocktail dresses. But should Countess Tartempion (French for 'thingamibob') drop by, with an *'ouf'* of relief, Eileen would let her *stylo* drop, rush over to the wardrobe and, after handing me *Le Monde* and a saucer of soft peanuts, say, 'We're just going round the corner for a coffee. I'll be back in an hour or so.' Goodness! I would think, have I become that much of a bore? Then Cyril telephoned and gave me Derek Jackson's number. The previous summer, when I had flown over to Europe to stay with the Moynihans in the Bouches-du-Rhône, Derek and Eileen had been there. Derek had offered to put me up in Paris on my way back to the States, but I had chosen to stay with Eileen in the rue du Bac, as I thought it would be cosier. Eileen had a brisk purposeful walk, kept her hair Topsy-style and whatever she wore looked as though it had been bought the day before. Although she had the reputation of being a high-powered intellectual, I did not find her at all intimidating. In fact, she gave the impression of being most anxious to please, to the extent that if someone made a joke, humorous or not, she would give a charitable laugh. I had met Derek many years before when he was married to Janetta, when they joined Cyril and me on a gastronomic tour of Bordeaux.

Before leaving Anne Moynihan that summer, Derek had offered to put me up in Paris on my way back to the States, but I had chosen to stay with Eileen, as I thought it would be cosier.

Later that year, Eileen had flown over to New York and I was in a position to add a few people to her intellectual list. Eileen was not at all embarrassed to be fêted in a railroad apartment, where the dominant room was the kitchen. She even invited some professional friends of her own. Auden climbed the dun stairs in his carpet slippers. Alan Pryce-Jones came as did Norman Mailer and Andy Warhol. The apartment was crowded. Everyone seemed at ease chattering and helping themselves to cheese out of the fridge. Stubs were light-heartedly thrown to the floor, and the following day the white lino was covered in burns and tiny stiletto dots, where the women, less fashionably-shod than Eileen (who wore flat, buckled Roger Vivier shoes), had ground their talons right through to the rotten boards beneath. But I didn't mind. People rang to say what a success that party had been and why didn't I do that sort of thing more often? Bowden Broadwater claimed it had been like a sabbatical do and had revived his undergrad days. Soon after, I called Andy Warhol, and asked if I might go round and watch him making one of his pornographic films. His apartment was close by. While Andy focused his camera on a nude couple writhing about on the couch, I spent the afternoon rather bored consuming whisky until he suddenly turned to me and said modestly that if I cared to be included in the film he could create a role for a grandmother. *A nude grandmother!* Petrified, I fled.

The Moynihans were also in New York. They took me with them on a trip to New Orleans. We had a lovely time visiting the Bayous and going to strip joints like the Club My-O-My, sparkling with unusual female impersonators. 'New Orleans' MOST UNIQUE NITE SPOT with the World's Most Beautiful Boys in Women's Attire.' It was trips like this that I missed when I got back to England.

Chapter XV

Living at the Ritz

Derek lived in a duplex house in the rue Louis-David. The sitting room led into a dark, walled garden. After inviting me out to dinner several times, he insisted I move in. In the mornings, Derek set off in a Deux Chevaux to the Bellevue laboratory on the outskirts of Paris where he did spectroscopy work, for which he was later awarded the Legion d'Honneur.

There was a delightful café on the corner of the rue Louis-David, where I would sit writing letters and drinking coffee, and a comfortable neighbourhood restaurant with *banquettes* where we often dined. Otherwise, Derek would bring back smoked salmon or caviar and lamb cutlets which he liked to cook. Then, after dinner, he washed up the dishes. The char, he said, might break a plate; when he could have bought up all the plates in China!

Derek did everything he could to please me. He filled my bedroom with red roses, those long-stalked, *perfect* roses that always remind me of hospital rooms. When I complained of the noise coming from the adjoining school playground, he would run upstairs and shout angrily down to the boys from his bedroom window. And once a week he came into my room and placed a wad of francs on the dressing table. It was an odd way of doing it. But who would have complained? It enabled me to have fittings at Christian Dior, Pierre Cardin and Yves St Laurent. Otherwise, I roamed the house pining after Alastair and reciting Edith Sitwell's 'Still Falls The Rain'.

Derek had a diverse character which is what made him interesting. Educated at Rugby, an establishment he jokingly referred to as 'Bugry', by profession a physicist, at Oxford he had been made Professor of Spectroscopy. He was also an expert amateur jockey and had ridden in the Grand National. He owned a stable of racehorses that were trained in Normandy. His Welsh father, Sir Charles Jackson, had been one of the founders of the *News of the World* and

Derek had inherited a fortune. He was fluent in both French and German. In the last World War he had been an air gunner in Bomber Command and, thanks to his association with Oxford's Professor Lindemann, later Lord Cherwell, Churchill's scientific adviser and statistician, put in charge of testing 'window' strips of metal foil dropped by our bombers to confuse the enemy's radar system. He had worked on ways of jamming radio transmissions directing German air defences and been decorated with the Legion of Merit by the United States. With all these attributes, he veered towards a Bohemian way of life which led to some odd foibles. He collected soap ends, a habit he may have picked up in France, where people hoard everything. He had been married four times: first, to Poppet John; then to Pamela Mitford; followed by Janetta Kee and Princess Ratibor, and he had left all four wives. I had not been in the house long before he wanted to make me his fifth. He had had a twin brother (who had been killed along with his showbiz mistress in a horse-drawn-sleigh accident at St Moritz) to whom he had been very attached. This, maybe, was the reason why he did not like living alone. Derek lost his temper easily and was always yapping at waiters. Of medium height, green-eyed and thin-lipped with brittle, grey hair and a strutting walk, he reminded me of a yapping Welsh terrier. He liked blurting out remarks, hoping to shock, like calling a church a 'God Box'. He was very generous when it came to taking groups of friends to Prunier's, Maxim's or the Ritz and whenever his friends came over from England, they immediately rang up knowing they would be given a smashing dinner. I have never known a more loyal man. When I told him that Robin Campbell had always been very snubbing, he was never invited again, although Derek liked him.

But with all that *'Bien entendu'*, *'Quoi! Quoi!'*, *'Ça va de soi'* and *'Bonjour Messieurs et Mesdames, c'est moi qui vous remercie'* as a shop door slams in your face, and their way of dismissing you with a *'Bon, allez'* when the conversation lags, as though you were the boring one, I have never been able to appreciate Parisians. There are exceptions, *bien sûr*. After all, I have now been living in France for over twenty years and I do have two good friends. But on the whole, they are family people, they prefer to stick to themselves, perhaps sharing W.'s sentiment (should a lot of drones come to dinner), 'What good are these people to my business?'

Derek also saw mostly English people. Nancy Mitford was always lively and amusing, and one night Meraud Guevara née Guinness ate a bad oyster at Prunier's. Derek was also a close friend of the Fascist leader, Oswald Mosley, who had married his former sister-in-law, Diana. He was, therefore, on cosy chatting terms with the Windsors and then there was Ethel de Croisset, a charming American lady he named *'la femme exquise'*. Otherwise, June Churchill or the homosexual youngest son of Lord Rosslyn, Hamish Erskine, Mary Campbell's brother, on whom Derek had once had a crush, might be staying in the damp spare bedroom. Then, with regard to theatre life, Sagan's *Le Cheval s'ennuit* was all the rage. Television speakerines grinned and wore Popish *perruques*. Commercials could be hilarious. *'Du Roquefort d'abord, du Roquefort d'accord'* still jingles away.

Gavin Young became easy to reach and at this stage even Eileen seemed to find me less of a bore. We would meet for lunch at the Brasserie Lipp and sit wedged between glamorous people tucking into pig's trotters. On sunny days, in a desperate attempt to obtain a tan, we frequented the rather sinister Bains Deligny, a swimming pool set in a boat moored on the Seine's Left Bank.

Once the Brooklyn couple had vacated my apartment, I planned to return to New York but Derek went on proposing marriage, so I finally gave in and accepted a topaz engagement ring.

A marriage can be founded on many things: mutual attraction or love, a breeding instinct, mutual snobbery and social climbing, a need for security and financial advancement – in the French tradition. It was not for love that I married Professor Jackson. But first I was taken to see his lawyer in Switzerland and asked to sign a document whereby I relinquished all claim on my future husband's millions. It seemed an odd formality instigated by someone professing himself to be so enamoured. *Enfin*, the deed done, a registry marriage took place in Lausanne with our two witnesses, the Moynihans. When the ceremony was over, the four of us partook of a celebration lunch. The wedding present was to be a Mercedes. Derek suffered from high blood pressure, which probably accounted for his sporadic rages, and he could not support the heat. But at my suggestion, we spent our July honeymoon in the Hôtel Baou that had just opened in Ramatuelle. Poppet and her third husband, a Dutchman, Pol, lived close by, and I had hoped that they might brighten up our evenings. Derek never went near the sea. He preferred to remain in his hotel room with a little calculating machine, doing spectroscopy work.

On the first day, when I drove to the beach, the Pols suddenly appeared with a picnic basket. We were lying on the sands discussing houses for sale, when I said, 'Goodness! How I'd love to have a house in the Midi.' And I remember Poppet went, 'Pouff! How could you afford a house here? They cost a packet.' Then I broke the news that I had married her ex-husband and I may be wrong, but I had the impression that our close friendship suddenly evaporated. We went on seeing each other, though, and from then on, perhaps imagining he might be my next victim, she kept a protective eye on Pol.

One evening, the Pols gave a cocktail party. Among the guests was a woman disparagingly named Virginia Creeper, who ran an estate agent in St Tropez. Derek had mentioned how much he enjoyed the sight of vineyards, so when he rushed back to Paris, I spent the rest of the honeymoon viewing suitably vineyardy properties for sale; we had decided to buy one in the Midi.

Although I would have preferred a house in a remoter region, we finally decided on an old *mas* in the forest behind Grimaud. A lawyer flew down from

Lausanne, bringing a wad of notes in a briefcase. In those days, to avoid paying property tax, the seller liked to be paid partly in cash so that the total sum of the property never got declared.

Every summer, Derek went to Deauville for the racing season, a suite being booked a year in advance in the luxurious Hôtel Normandy, which resembled a prison. Though Derek usually had a horse running, he never bet. When not sitting in the grandstand, he roamed the paddock chatting with his trainer. And I am no gambler, even if I have money to lose, so, rather than attend the races, I preferred to have a knock-up with the hotel tennis pro or swim from a crowded Deauville beach. The afternoon Derek bought six yearlings for £12,000, I happened to wander into Van Cleef. The *vendeuse* was a close friend of Derek's. She greeted me warmly and brought out a tray of jewellery on which lay a magnificent square-cut emerald. Used to dealing with rich men's wives and seeing my approbation, she intimated that the jewel could be put down on Derek's account. Perhaps wrongly, I decided on the setting of a man's gold signet ring. A month later, I remember so well going to the Place Vendôme to collect the emerald and walking away from Van Cleef with this beautiful ring on my finger to board a crowded bus, and wondering whether, should my hand strike the handrail, the stone would crack. Then Derek and I set about finding a less dark and damp house. But we had totally opposing tastes. There was one lovely apartment with a terrace looking on to the Seine for a million francs. Derek thought the price outrageous. It also had a view of Nôtre-Dame, the epitome of all God Boxes. So when the Louis-David house was sold for double Derek had paid five years before, we had nowhere to live and we moved into a suite at the Ritz. A salon separated our rooms. A British cat breeder sent over another Abyssinian and I collected Melanie from the airport. One day, passing a pet shop on the Quai des Fleurs, I saw a baby coati shut up in a box and bought Folie, so named after Georges Bernier's prophecy, on hearing of my marriage to W., 'C'est de la folie totale.' Though Folie did once get on to the roof and frighten an elderly lady by entering her bedroom window, and Mell kept running into the corridor and entering other people's suites, the animals settled down well to a life of luxury.

One day I went into the Bois de Boulogne with the floor waiter who helped me give Folie a run, but when we put her up a tree, she turned out to be retarded and could not climb down, and this handicap eventually led to her undoing.

The Ritz breakfast, oddly enough, was always a disappointment. The coffee never tasted freshly ground. So I bought a gas ring and grinder, and made my own. Derek had, as I have mentioned, his eccentricities. Instead of ringing for the floor waiter at drinks time, he preferred to buy a bottle of whisky, bring it in and only rang when he wanted some ice to be brought.

One evening, we took Jim and Larry to dinner at Maxim's. Afterwards we all went to a nightclub. Jim and I were rudely chattering across Derek who lost his temper, grabbed our two heads and cracked them together like a pair of walnuts. Whereupon I took Derek's hand and bit into his thumb. The next tiff took place at the Ritz. This time I snapped at my husband's lip. A doctor had to be summoned and Derek went about with a bandaged chin so that his loyal ex-wife, Janetta, assuming Folie to be the culprit, said to him, 'You ought to have that vicious animal put down.'

I wrote to Cyril: 'Tell Janetta from me she's a silly bitch. People who talk of putting animals down ought to be put down themselves. The coati is a sweet, docile little animal who hardly dares bite into a banana, let alone a pair of thin lips, and prefers snails, anyway.'

Mummy wrote to say that a friend of hers had read in a paper that 'Derek had been bitten by your coati and he was going about with a patch on his mouth. I hope it is nothing serious . . .'

I then decided I would like to own a Balthus and, with Derek's approval, I went to the Balthus Gallery in Paris, but there were none for sale. A Balthus, they said, was always bought in advance by some collector. It was Jim who finally found one for sale in New York — one of those sensual young ladies wearing a *négligé* and bright red slippers, reclining on a Récamier. Although I had seen a photograph of the painting before it was shipped over, when the young lady arrived she bore such a strong resemblance to a youthful Yvonne Hamilton that a month later, leaving Folie in the care of the floor waiter who lived in a squalid hotel off the Champs-Elysées, I had to traipse with the picture all the way back to New York, travelling first class on *La France*, a gigantic new liner with so many bars and elevators I could never find my cabin. (It was later transformed into a Caribbean cruise ship.) The same New York gallery took back the Balthus and gave me $24,000. It would now be worth a fortune.

Dressed by Dior and Cardin, I found I had become far more popular and got taken on a round of parties. Charlie took me to a party given by Drue Heintz where one saw Sagan sitting dolefully alone without anyone to talk to and Norman Mailer went round shadow-boxing. Bowden took me to the Rolos. Earl Macgrath gave a party. Bob included me in a dinner for Isaiah Berlin and Nelson Aldrich. Then I flew to Palm Beach for the weekend and got back to Paris exhausted.

I may be wrong but I got the impression that '*mon ami*' Jim had expected to be given a commission on the first Balthus deal, but I do not think it was the reason that, apart from a brief encounter in the Deux Magots, we did not meet for fifteen years, when I was living in Seine-et-Marne and Jim drove down for dinner. As soon as he entered the walled garden, he asked, on seeing a superb cherry tree dripping with fruit, for a ladder, which he mounted, and the tree was summarily stripped. Teeny Duchamp, the painter's wife, also came to dinner. Afterwards Jim drove her home to see her collection of surrealist paintings. The next day he rang to thank me, adding that he had given the cherries to his housekeeper.

Derek and I went on living in the Ritz with the animals and *Tristan und Isolde* blaring away on the stereo, even after the management had retaliated, and not even Derek's rages would rid our suite of the sound of clogs overhead.

Then, having arranged with him that Mummy and Aunty Greta be relieved of any further money worries, and that each should receive a life settlement, I packed my offspring into the car and drove to the Midi to install myself with an oil lamp, a bed, a gas stove and fridge in the *mas*, and set about finding a builder to raise the roof on one side and build on a bedroom that would have a view of the surrounding valley. Derek flew down at weekends and stayed either in Grimaud or in the residence de la Pinède, a luxury hotel in St Tropez, until one day he broke a leg running into the Place Vendôme to hail a taxi, and I returned to Paris, when my diary callously notes: 'Alone at the Ritz. What bliss!'

While Derek was in hospital with his leg in plaster, Eileen introduced me to the Marquis de Ségur who invited me out to dinner. When we left the restaurant, the Marquis asked me back to his apartment for coffee and a liqueur for the sole purpose, it turned out, of seducing me on his sofa. Alas, he was not exactly an *'homme fatal'* and, after a lengthy struggle with my black Cardin boots that reached up to the thighs, panting with exhaustion, he gave up.

When Derek came out of hospital we both agreed on an apartment in the rue Jean-Goujon, off the Avenue Montaigne. Derek bought it, whereupon, to his horror, I found a decorator who set about distempering the walls in violent colours; for apart from a tiny Corot, he owned a rather dull collection of Impressionist paintings that would admittedly have looked more remarkable when seen against a muted background. But we were never to live in the rue Jean-Goujon. By then, to quote Cyril, Derek had found his Katharine Parr. There is no doubt that a lot of money can be deleterious. It can cause those who own a great deal to feel slightly superior and a world apart from the menial side of existence. Though I sometimes regret it, I escaped this fate. For once the apartment was furnished and ready for habitation, Derek and I agreed to an amicable separation which led to a divorce. I was bequeathed the *mas* and Derek took a sixth wife, Marie-Christine Reille, who remained with him for the rest of his life.

Two years later, I received a letter from out of the blue:

It might come to you as a surprise to hear from me . . . a lot of time has passed since we met in Paris at the Ritz. At the moment I am travelling with some English friends from London to Bangkok and I can assure you it is a long drive. It gives me plenty of time to think and I think quite often. I'll be going back to Japan after Bangkok. Who would have thought I was going to end up in such a remote country . . .? Sometimes I ask myself what you are doing and your last book, *A Love Match*, just gave me an idea what is going on in your country house. I also counted how often you used words like 'disgusting' or 'ridiculous'. It's quite funny and an experience to read a book by a person I know. Also you might not know that I worked two years at Claridge's as a floor waiter and I liked the place very much. I saw your former husband occasionally but we didn't have much to say to each other. I wonder if he even remembered me. It didn't sound like it! I also bought *Born Losers* and I prefer it to the other one. Your coatis are mentioned and I would very much like to know how they are doing . . .

Let me hope your sense of humour is still the same and you have forgiven me for these unfortunate mistakes I made. Peter.

Chapter XVI

Grimaud

The Mas de Colombier was a typical Provençal farmhouse, elongated and built of blocks of pinkish sandstone. The ceilings were low and oak-beamed, and the walls were whitewashed. The floors had octagonal tiles. As it was high up, water came from an abundant source. Then, there was no electricity and it was lit by oil lamps. The *bourgeois* French can be very helpful when new occupants take over their property. The previous owners had moved down into the valley, and I remember so well that first, cold month of March their driving up in a raging *mistral* in order to bring me a paraffin stove to heat the bedroom and literally battling their way across the terrace.* Being isolated high up in the forest, they advised me to keep a gun in the bedroom, as they had done, in case of night prowlers.

The Colombier looked on to a valley and had an extensive view of vineyards surrounded by low, overlapping mountains. At dusk, when the sun set behind the mountains, the entire horizon glowed. The terrace was bordered by a rosemary hedge and on one side stretched a line of cypresses as protection against the *mistral*. There were six hectares of land, most of it forest.

We took our meals at a bistro table beneath a eucalyptus tree or in the shade of a mulberry, and dotted about were clumps of lavender, sweet-smelling verbena, white clumps of marguerites and little yellow flowers whose

---

* Since then much has changed in the Midi, including the climate. The *mistral* rarely lasts long enough to drive away the clouds. Instead, a cold Tramontin wind blows, there is incessant rain and in summer it is no longer necessary to water the garden every evening, as one did in those light-hearted days.

petals closed at dusk. A steep, winding dust road led up to the *mas*. And at the back rose the forest. Those prepared for a steep climb could reach the summit and glimpse the Mediterranean. The surroundings were so peaceful that all one ever heard was an occasional tractor tilling the vines, and myriad birds the moment the shutters were opened in the morning. There was one I called the Woof-Woof bird; another made a strange guttural sound, like the creaking of a limb. There were red-crested speckled woodpeckers, merles, pheasants and cuckoos. In spring, the silence of the night would be broken by the magical sound of nightingales calling to one another.

The only other dwelling to be seen in the far distance was a large property inhabited by an old peasant (always clad in black), her sluttish daughter and drunken son-in-law, who owned the surrounding vineyards; from them, for seventy-five francs a year, I rented a meadow where the laundry got hung between two mulberry trees. In fact, the first person to come up to the *mas* one Sunday was the drunken son-in-law to show me the red *bornes* separating our properties. He led the way into the forest. I followed with Mell and Folie. Suddenly, he stopped and suggested we lie down on a pile of bracken. When rejected, he said oafishly, 'So, you're *indisposée* today, Madame. Some other time, perhaps,' and left me to follow a trail of alcohol back to the house.

The *mas* was still barely furnished, when at dawn one morning I was awoken by the sound of pebbles striking the shutters of my bedroom window. Pulling on a blue kaftan, I went downstairs with Folie draped round me like a stole, her paws clinging to my hair, and opened the door to see Bernard Frank dressed in a dinner jacket, standing on the terrace. He had just come from a nightclub, where he had been carousing with Françoise Sagan and her faithful '*bande*' of which, at that time, he was the principal jester. He must have been well received, for he dismissed the car he had come in and entered the *mas*, where he remained on and off for the next thirteen years, using it as his *résidence secondaire*.

I have had the good fortune to have loved and lived with two exceptionally talented and witty writers. Though neither of them could have been described as an Adonis, they both had immense success with women and were difficult to live with. Both had had traumatic childhoods. Cyril's mother had abandoned her 'sprat' to join the man she loved in South Africa and Bernard had to flee Paris with his parents, during the German occupation, and seek refuge in the Auvergne.

I had first met Bernard with Eileen Geist. Dropping into the rue du Bac before or after luncheon one day, there was Bernard lying dressed, corpulent and flushed, a cigar in his mouth, stretched out on Eileen's quilt. Should she say, 'Another whisky?' the response was immediate: '*Volontiers!*' Eileen assiduously gave him all her attention and when not refilling his glass, she held out an ashtray at arm's length to catch the cigar ash before it hit her quilt. Bernard was then very teddy-bear-like; even his hair seemed woolly. He had written six books and all of them lay on the bedside table. He was living round the corner from Eileen with Françoise Sagan, and he and Eileen were discussing all the fascinating people who had been at Sagan's party the previous evening. Suddenly, as though noticing me for the first time, Eileen turned and said, 'What are you doing this evening? I'm busy and Bernard hates having to spend an evening alone.' In those days, being far more puritanical, I did not relish sitting perched up half the night on one of Régine's bar stools. 'What a pity,' said Eileen, 'then you won't do.' And they went on discussing the party.

When Bernard turned up on the terrace he was staying with Sagan in a villa she had rented in the Parc St Tropez. Her sister was there, an actor and a film director's wife, and a few days later there was a big party given for Françoise's birthday on Madame Hélène Rochas's yacht, where the dancer, Jacques Chazot, was the most amusing *invité*.

At that time, Bernard was drinking a lot and constantly falling over. He suffered from slight aphasia and sometimes his conversation became so garbled he made practically no sense. Once, after an evening in a nightclub with Sagan, he got a taxi to bring him back and was dropped off at the bottom of the hill; I looked out of the window at dawn to see him climbing up to the *mas à quatre pattes*. The first time Françoise came up, I remember her doing a funny imitation of a cripple, hobbling about the tiles with the aid of a stick. There was no hint of reproach, she was merely trying to warn 'dear Bernie' of what might happen, if he did not sober up. And in fact, some months later, he did have a serious stroke and was taken into St Tropez hospital.

Both Sagan and Bernard had tremendous charm. Seeing them seated side by side, like siblings, they reminded me of a pair of oddly matched *perroquets*, one a slight blonde and chirrupy, the other a big, brown, ponderous bird. Bernard had many conflicting sides to his character. Though not always courteous, he was nevertheless still then an ardent handkisser. He could also be very paternal and give sound advice. He was surprisingly uncritical and loyal to his friends, and should you condemn anyone, he'd retaliate by picking on your own hideous faults. His main interests were politics and literature. He was singularly lacking in curiosity about anything else, unless it directly concerned himself. He was a terrible spendthrift. Whenever he had earned a little money writing articles for magazines he would immediately take one to an expensive restaurant.

I had always found flattery suspect. No problem there. It was soon taken for granted that I was merely a *'connasse'* and that a lot of the time my eyes resembled 'glaring prairie oysters'. I had never been able to tolerate a bore. One thing he taught me, there can be far worse handicaps than being a bore, particularly when he was indulging in his poltergeist act, skimming plates across the terrace. Afterwards, he would simply say, 'I am a *coléreux*, but my rages quickly blow over . . .' – like the crockery is all I can say. Bernard had what is known as *un bon coeur*. He was a very lovable man, but when with a woman he cared about, he could be very sadistic.

The morning of his arrival on the terrace, I went into the village to telephone Eileen, who gave the impression then of having some kind of ownership and having taken on a motherly role with regard to Bernard. When I related that he had turned up in the early hours blotto and was now asleep in my bed, she said, 'Poor Bernard, when he comes to, he won't know where he is or who you are!' But when I got back, he related that ever since our first meeting on Eileen's quilt, he had had me in mind as a possible future mistress. What could it have been? My woollies? A waning, come-hither look? The fact that I was Eileen's friend? What is a friend, after all? One joined to another in mutual intimacy and benevolence, according to the dictionary. Not an enemy. Well, that applied. Eileen was not likely to visit you, should you be very ill, as Jocelyn would, bringing you some home-cooked dish to revive your appetite. But Eileen would certainly call up after an operation to find out if you had pulled through. Her mornings were spent on the telephone. Let's say she was a delightful, fair-weather friend.

The morning Bernard turned up on the terrace, main water was being installed. A trench was being dug all the way up the hill to contain the pipes and a lorry load of whistling Arabs drove up at seven every morning. When later that day I went out, carrying a trayload of vodka, glasses, lemons and a tin of beef consommé – all the requirements of a bullshot* – followed by Bernard crumpled and unshaven, the Arabs stopped digging and, leaning on their shovels, looked in our direction, as much as to say, 'There's a lucky pasha who knows how to get through a hot day with the least possible effort!' They decided to do the same and, squatting on the grass, brought out luncheon packages of sardines, bars of chocolate and bottles of Coca-Cola. As Bernard swayed across the terrace to get into the car on our way out to lunch, I said, 'They must be thinking, Where on earth did she pick him up?' And I went on laughing all the way down the hill, until we reached Grimaud village where Bernard asked me to buy him a box of cigars.

After mains water, electricity had to be installed. The electricians swarmed all over the house, so that Bernard moved into a beamed *cabanon* just below the terrace. He would tiptoe up to the house as though he felt in the way. In those days, there was never a cross word.

Then central heating was installed. I became demented on days the workmen did not turn up because they had been sent to complete some other job. So we

---

* The perfect hangover cure.

decided to take on a budding architect to harry the men in my stead – a frequent custom in the Midi, where the work is generally slipshod.

Carelli sought out rare objects for those willing to pay for his impeccable taste. His aunt ran the antique shop in Grimaud, where I had bought old glasses, Provençal coffee cups and carafes, one blue and one golden, like the carafe in Degas's 'Absinthe'.

Carelli would come hurtling up the hill in a Deux Chevaux and, leaping out, with an eager smile on his face, would come running across the terrace like some newly appointed lieutenant, exclaiming, 'How I love this house! The view is so superb.' He then drew up a plan for converting two barns at the far end of the *mas* into a kitchen, and another bedroom and bathroom that were to become Bernard's quarters. Carelli then dismissed my *equipe* and called in another builder, carpenter and electrician, and gained a commission from each.

One afternoon, Mell and Folie were lying sprawled out in the sun, when a lorry mounted the hillside, bringing the residue of my furniture that had been shipped over from the States, and Bernard helped me unwrap the china and books that he assiduously arranged in alphabetical order in the new bookshelves in the sitting room.

'I'm not very affectionate, am I?' I said.

'Oh yes, *you are*,' Bernard contradicted. 'I don't like cloying women. Anyway, from now on, this is going to be my workroom.' Alas, not for nothing had I been divorced on grounds of incompatability. The sitting room, with its newly built-in bookshelves and Provençal fireplace, black plaque of shepherdesses, sphinx fire-dogs and curtains drawn, as in the best parlour for guests, was going to remain a sitting room.

Bernard like to gamble. On some evenings, we would drive into Cannes. My diary records: 'Lose money gambling in the Casino. Begin to feel attached to B.F. My birthday. B.F. gives me one of his old pullovers. Have to support B.F. Blue sky fleeced with rain. Today he was sulky from the start. Would I lend him 200 francs? Am accused of being *avare*. The plumber and the mason arrive. We all clear out the garage where Bernard's new room is going to be. The gardener has planted more almond trees. Compressor all day. B. has written to his tailor and to his lawyer, sending money on account. Insulting letters both.

'If you devoted as much time to writing your book,' I say, 'there might be some point.'

Wants to know what his new room will be like. Can he have grey walls? Discuss what's for dinner. Hear a car, the builders burst in. Very aggressive. B. pretends there's no drink. Offers them beer. The ugly one says, 'No whisky or vodka?' Bernard goes on swilling. I say, 'You've got that idiotic look on your face.' He says, 'If you're going to be disagreeable, I'm off to bed.' Saturday keeps to his room when seen slinking in and out, mutters, '*Bonjour*'. Sunday wasn't much better. Comes upstairs. Sees all the animals on the bed, goes out again. *Gigot* for lunch.'

Two tragedies occurred about this time. Mell broke a leg being chased up a tree by the builder's *chien de chasse* and Folie disappeared into the forest, never to be seen again — chased and killed by the same dog, I presumed. For dogs are a coati's worst enemy. And the poor little beast couldn't climb. I was terribly distressed. So more coatis were flown over from a New York pet shop. I had asked for a couple, hoping they would breed, but they both turned out to be males. One was reddish brown and I called him Nig. The other was sandy coloured. As soon as he was let out of his travelling box, he made a systematic tour of the terrace, grubbing for slugs and snails. He was so auntyish that Bernard named him Tantine. Later, he became so chubby that I called him Fatty Fat Fat. When one picked him up it was like hugging a little bear. All coatis are intrigued by anything scented; he would scuttle into my bathroom, get hold of the soap and scrabble it all over his ringed tail, forming a thick mousse. Both of them ran about free and sometimes they disappeared into the forest for days, causing many sleepless nights. But I would always leave the front door ajar so that I would know when they got back, when they would clamber up the stairs, give my hand a lick and then curl up on the bed.

From the start, Bernard made it clear that he had other ladies lined up, awaiting his return to Paris. When Sagan drove up unexpectedly one autumn evening and, after comparing the view to that of an Indian jungle, drove away taking Bernard and his four suitcases, I let them go. Then I polished off the rest of the whisky, drove furiously down the hill and landed in a ditch. The next day, the car had to be hauled out by a crane. On the opposite side of the valley, a track led up to a run-down farmhouse hidden behind a copse of cork oaks, where Thérèse lived with her husband, Joseph, and their four children. Thérèse came from Aix-en-Provence. She had very green eyes and brown, sturdy legs, and she always came to clean wearing a sleeveless print dress, walking down her side of the valley and up to the *mas*. Thérèse knew how to mend a fuse, remove any stain and foretell the weather from the way Joseph's hair behaved.

'It's very *bouclé* today,' she'd say. 'It's sure to rain.'

Thérèse never spoke evil of anyone, even when they were caught out gathering her home-grown vegetables. 'It's human nature. What do you expect?' was her philosophy. Thérèse never flinched on entering my bedroom to see the tiles chipped after a hammer had hurtled through the window or the bed collapsed with castors rolling in all directions, her attitude being that so long as there were no broken teeth or bones to be swept up, everything was all right. And once, after a tap had been left running in my bathroom (Bernie's attempt to drown Mummy, one could say) Thérèse made no comment. She merely hauled a pail up the stairs and spent the afternoon swilling. It was only towards the end of the affair and she arrived to find the dishwasher overturned, and all the crockery in smithereens on the kitchen floor, that she admitted to being scared.

When not tending thirty hectares of vines for an absentee landlord, Joseph came up and gardened. He always had something cheerful to say.

'Il fait beau aujourd'hui,' he said, even if a mistral raged. His laugh was infectious and made you feel that life was worth living. Joseph liked to tipple and, at the end of a day's gardening, he would come into the kitchen to have a chat and I brought out the bidon of wine.

When not bottling, cooking or sewing for her family, Thérèse often had relatives to stay. It was a mystery where everyone slept, there being only two bedrooms in their farmhouse. Joseph's retarded brother slept in the stable with the mule. Should they have an excessive overflow and I was alone, Thérèse and Joseph came over and slept in the mas. I enjoyed their company, even if, like all the locals, they repeated everything four times over and, after their departure, the spare room remained redolent of copulating beasts. It was, however, preferable to the stench of stale tobacco or face powder. They never left the mattress covered in coffee stains or the walls spattered with mosquitoes, as more sophisticated guests sometimes did. They would arrive early in the evening and, before going to bed, talk in front of the fire, then leave early in the morning, when their alarm bell went. I became very fond of the whole family and often gave them things. Should I, for some reason, walk over to their farm, after visiting their mule, the pigs and the four chained dogs, I would go into their kitchen to find everyone rigged out in one of my discarded garments. The eldest daughter would be wearing my pretty Capri sandals, Joseph that old Isle of Aran pullover and the youngest son, Joel, looked so dashing in my Mexican sombrero that I often felt tempted to ask for it back.

On a clear day, when Joseph was tilling the vines, one could hear him cursing his mule, and if it wasn't for the echo of the buzz-saw carving wood, or the children's voices in autumn as they gathered cèpes or pine cones for a fire, the quiet of the valley might have become unendurable.

In the early days, when I went to England, they would take care of the cats, until one year Mell ate their pet canary as it flew out of its cage; and though Joseph admired Mell's ability as a rat catcher, she was never allowed on to the farm again.

Chapter XVII

Life at the *Mas*

Soon after Bernard went off with Sagan, I found myself being courted by a Frenchman engaged in the construction of HLMs (*Habitations à Loyer Modéré*) in Sainte Maxime. Monsieur Boucarat was a sturdy-looking man with a raffish disposition. He had worked for the CIA in Vietnam where, according to him, his wife had fallen in love with Graham Greene. Boucarat would bring his friends over for the weekend. They would clear the gravel off the terrace and play *boules*. In the evenings, we dined out somewhere on the coast and usually ended up in a nightclub. On Sunday, he came to dinner and left the *mas* around midnight, claiming that throughout all his years in the Midi, he had never known it to be so cold. Sure enough, early next morning, I opened the front door to find the valley completely enveloped in snow. Icicles hung from the trees and there was not a branch to be seen. It was a beautiful sunny day and the snow glistened. The electricity was cut and the pipes had frozen. In order to make coffee, I went out and scooped up the snow in a saucepan.

Joseph had built a large cage for the coatis beneath four umbrella pines on the hill behind the *mas*, but when I went out to rescue them the snow was so deep that it was impossible to wade through it, so I had to climb up to the cage on all fours and carry each coati, Lorenz-style, on my back into the house. And there we remained for days, Mell, Nig, Tantine and myself, reading Balzac with a bottle of whisky beside the bed and sunlight streaming into the bedroom.

The snow was beginning to thaw when who should come toiling up the hill but Joseph, bringing me a loaf of bread. Soon after, the shepherd appeared, pushing a bicycle. He stood beaming beneath the bedroom window, tenderly holding something wrapped in a dishcloth and shouted up, 'Look what I've brought you, Madame.' Goodness. I thought, what could it be, his genitals?

The shepherd lived down in the valley and often came up with his flock to graze in the meadow or on the hill. In those days, it was the custom, just before Christmas, for him to take each landowner a *gigot* and that is what he had brought me.

Diary

Alone with Nig and Tantine, *brun et blonde*, and a female Toute Petite, kept in the lavatory; too cold to put her out . . . Mell is downstairs on the Récamier. Bernard is with Sagan. I have now adapted to being alone. Coatis let out one at a time. They sometimes stay out three days. When they come back they clamber into the niche on the terrace. This morning I could hear Nig scratching, so I knew he was back.

My day. Wake up at five, turn on the heating, make coffee, feed Mell and Toute Petite. Am reading *Cousin Pons*; write; go out and shop. Scrutinise watch a good deal. Afternoons Thérèse comes, I light a fire round five in the evening; take a librium with my *mélange* of Scotch, lie beside fire and read; eat. This year I am fifty-three; think of that . . . It's getting serious. My debts are now all paid.

One evening, the postman cycled up the hill with a telegram which read: '*Arrive demain 8 am. Attends votre présence à la gare. T'embrasse. Bernard.*' And off I went, the squaw at dawn to the station.

We were driving back along the coast, when who should be crossing the street on his way to work but Monsieur Boucarat, who saw me at the wheel of the Mercedes, with Bernard in the passenger seat, and that was the end of him. Months later, on the port of St Tropez, he stuck his head out of a car merely to boast that he was deeply involved with a Countess and drove off, adamantly standoffish.

When Bernard arrived from Paris, he always went on a *régime*. In the evenings, we drank one whisky each and a *carafe* of red wine with our dinner. At drinks time, he'd pace the sitting room, a glass in his hand, his head crowned with my barette, telling me about the women who had been important in his life, while I, seated on the *banquette*, watched him spellbound. He had a habit of pulling his hair over his brow, going over to the mirror and patting his cheeks with an invisible powder puff, parodying Sagan. Like her, he was very difficult to understand, not because he talked so rapidly but because he mumbled.

I am not at all nocturnal. Seven am is my finest hour and so much the better if it is still pitch dark outside. Then I go down and prepare coffee, hot milk and buttered toast, which I carry up to bed. Bernard has his breakfast later.

In the early days, as soon as he awoke, he would come up to my room and ask if I had slept well. I could usually interpret his mood from the pace of his footsteps on the tiles. If he came in full tilt it was to impart discomforting news. The electricity had been left on downstairs all night, or the stray black Tom had leapt through the kitchen window and gone off with the bread. Leaden footsteps meant he had come to tell me how badly he had slept. Then I went down and prepared his breakfast – Lapsang suchong with a *biscotte*.

Once his new quarters had been built on at the far end of the *mas* next to the kitchen, he preferred to walk on to the terrace and, the distance being shorter, shout up, '*Deuxième service, s'il vous plaît!*' Sometimes, it took so long before his shutters opened that I feared he might be ill. For, like Daddy's, Bernard's health was an all-absorbing topic.

In the beginning, it was I who did the shopping. Bernard participated in other ways. In the evenings, he drenched himself hosing the garden. He seemed to enjoy stacking the dishwasher and defrosting the icebox, grilling cutlets on the barbecue and making pressure cooker stews. It was Bernard who prepared the evening drinks and laid the dinner table, and later, when the swimming pool was built, though he was never known to set foot in it, he became the beach boy. Dressed in a blue kaftan, he circled the pool with a net scooping up dead mice and saving the lives of struggling *grenouilles*. In fact, he could have made a living that way. I liked to shop early, before too many people were about. We shopped in Cogolin, a wealthy little town renowned for hand-spun tapestries and briar pipes, the briar being hacked in the surrounding forest. Only much later, with a socialist mayor and increasing hordes of tourists did the *place*, lined with giant palms, become a parking lot. Opposite the town hall was a very good butcher. People came in from St Tropez to buy his meat. Should I go in early, I'd come upon the butcher's son perched on the kerb in squelchy, yellow, plastic sandals, wiping his hands on a bloody, striped apron. Should I say, 'What is there good today?' looking down his nose he'd reply coldly, '*Il y a un peu de tout ici, Madame.*' No matter, I always bought the same thing.

'*Deux côtelettes dans le filet, s'il vous plaît.*' The lamb came from Sisteron and was particularly delicious.

In the Casino, where they bowed you in and out with *Bonjour Mesdames Messieurs c'est moi qui vous remercie*' and where everything cost a few cents less than in the other co-ops, the manager would watch every move one made due to shop-lifting. And while piling up your carton, the *serveuse* would go on repeating, '*Ensuite, Madame. Ensuite.*'

At the entrance to Cogolin was a fishmonger. His fish came from Toulon, so he said. He was a very jolly man and had a habit of swinging a big fish by the tail over his head and slapping it on the slab, with the joyous cry of '*Oopla . . .*'

The shopping over, when getting into the car I was sometimes waylaid by a pair of gipsies, balancing babies, who haunted the *place*. Grabbing hold of my arm, one would cry, '*Montre-moi ta main, ma jolie!*' And once addressing the street, she shrieked, '*Regardez comme elle est belle!*' And with that compliment ringing in my head, without giving a sou, I had crashed into gear and raced off to Grimaud, where we bought the newspapers. The woman who ran the bookshop was a likeable old witch who always had a petticoat strap showing and when she smiled, all one saw were two front teeth with a gap between. The newspapers arrived by bus at the bottom of the hill and she then had to carry them up on her back to the *librairie* which gave on to the Place Vieille where the villagers played *boules*. Should I arrive after midday, she might be frying sardines on a gas ring. If there were no English newspapers, she'd say dolefully, as though attending the undertakers, 'I don't know what can be keeping them. They haven't come in yet.'

When Bernard heard the car charge up the hill, he would come on to the terrace in his dressing gown and say, 'You haven't forgotten my Micky? My Craven?' or whatever it was he awaited, and then he went back to bed taking Mell. Abyssinians are great hunters. Scarcely a day passed when Mell did not bring in a lizard, a mole or a field mouse. She would kill her victim with one paw stroke; all that remained might be a tail or a flurry of feathers on the tiles. Should she bring in a rabbit, I'd skin and cook it for her. In the evenings, when Bernard got up to go into the kitchen, Mell would leap off the *banquette*, run ahead and stand beside the fridge, her tail quivering with anticipation until he had stacked her dish with Ronron, Whiskas or Mitou. While eating, she had a habit of peering over her shoulder, in case the stray Tom that haunted the terrace suddenly leapt through the window. When not hungry, she flicked her hind paws at the dish in a series of scuffing movements, as though the food were excrement.

Apart from Bernard's friends, like Sagan or Claude Perdriel, owner of *Le Nouvel Observateur*, the only people we saw were the Pols, who belonged to what we jokingly referred to as 'the villa set', a snobbish élite dotted about the coast, or we would lunch with Pippa and Peter Forster, a journalist on the *Evening Standard*. They lived at La Garde-Freinet, where Pippa had created a typical English garden, with flowerbeds and grassy inclines. Peter did the cooking and whenever we went to lunch we would arrive to find him purple in the face, grooved to a chaotic kitchen, tippling. His menus were rustic. Once he had prepared a *brandade* on to which were stacked a pile of mashed potatoes and fried eggs. We ate under a trellis in the garden and it was always agreeable. When alone, I might lunch in Grimaud with a Danish beauty who had been married to John Churchill. She had a little Welsh terrier called Jackson that liked to leap into the swimming pool on a hot day to cool off.

June Churchill was the first person to invite herself to stay. She had been a close friend during the Weidenfeld crisis and had advised me to give him that same treatment she had given Randolph: refuse to sleep with him for three months and then have him followed, she said. And when I was married to Derek, she took me with her to Majorca, where Sonia Melchett had lent her a villa by the sea. June remained in bed with the same sentimental record on the repeat and only got up for meals. She came to stay in the Midi in the first week of October just after she had had a breast operation, and she was infatuated with a possessive Greek shipowner. The taxidriver having lost the way, she arrived late at night and immediately asked to have a fire lit in her room. She rejected any Provençal-type cooking and had a horror of food cooked in butter. What she preferred was a simple meal of cold ham with potatoes baked in their jackets. During meals, we would gossip about our quixotic pasts, which seemed to annoy Bernard. One evening, during dinner, he was telling us about a dachshund he once owned called Joke that had had dirty habits. He'd punish Joke, he said, by thrusting the dog's head down a water closet. When I appeared to be shocked, June calmly said, 'He's boasting, to give the impression he's macho.' The idea struck me as so funny that I couldn't stop laughing. 'Are you drunk?' she kept repeating irritably. 'It's not that funny.'

One evening she was taking a shower when I heard her scream and, draped in a towel, she went hurtling down the stairs screaming for Bernard. Apparently, while taking a *douche*, a toad had leapt out of the *bidet*. Bernard coped very well. He came upstairs with a broom and swept it off her terrace, and as the two remained drinking in the sitting room while I prepared the dinner, my jealous disposition was exacerbated; the rice got burnt and, without consulting me, Bernard opened the last bottle of Derek's vintage Bordeaux. The atmosphere grew so tense that June disappeared up to her room. Around midnight, just below her window on the moonlit terrace, there was a scene; in spite of my cries for help, June preferred not to hear, so that I was dragged by the hair down some stone steps and flung into a tomato patch.

In the morning, no one commented on my black eye. In her hurry to depart, June left a gold evening bag and some dancing pumps in the cupboard. Was it a reproach as we hadn't left the house? It is doubtful if, Freudian fashion, it meant that she was anxious to return. When I drove her into St Raphael, June said, while waiting for the Blue Train, 'I think you ought to put a door between my room and the *bidet*. It isn't everyone who likes to have a view of a *bidet* when in bed.' In that way she was conventional.* Later, reports of the visit drifted

---

*A few years later, when I was spending the summer in London, we arranged to meet for lunch. June cancelled at the last moment, saying, 'I don't think we have anything in common.' A belated discovery, but in a sense, true. June was very likeable, but inclined to be humourless and quick-tempered about something quite trifling. She was very level-headed and appreciated the importance of money. What we had in common was old lovers.

back. I had become so antisocial that whenever I heard a car coming up the hill I hid behind trees. But then I had good reason to, for I was being pursued by French *douanes*.

In the Sixties, shops in Paris liked to be paid in dollars, as they reduced the tax. Derek bought practically everything at a reduced price, including the Mercedes. But after six months one was supposed to pay customs, the car then being rated second-hand. Unknown to me, he had neglected to pay this duty, and while June was staying two customs' officers came up and confiscated the car.

In those days, *gendarmes* were far more insulting, even with foreigners. They were capable of giving you an alcohol test at seven in the morning, knowing full well you were stone-cold sober. Everyone dreaded being stopped for speeding. One hot summer's day, I was driving full speed to Paris (I was still living at the Ritz) when I was stopped near Dijon by a bareheaded *gendarme* who demanded I pay a fine right away, so I pretended I had no money.

Show me your handbag, he said aggressively, whereupon I accelerated.

The car was traced by its number plate. I received a summons to appear in court and it looked as though I really were in for it. I went to the Faubourg St Honoré to see the head of the *gendarmerie*, a Monsieur Douce, who lived up to his name. Assuming me to be one of the idle rich, he asked how I spent my day, and offered me coffee and a liqueur. The situation was saved by the fact that the *gendarme* was not only without his *kepi* but unaccompanied, as they always hunt in pairs, and he could well have been an impostor. A month later, two *gendarmes* came up to the *mas* and took a further statement. And that was the end of the affair.

I was always having trouble with the Mercedes. When Bernard and I were staying with François Michel, a musicologist who lived at Montaigre, in the L'Ain, our host sent us off one day to the charming provincial town of Belley* to fetch an *ombre Chevalier* he had ordered for a luncheon party. We parked in the main street in front of the Hôtel Chabert and went into the bar. Suddenly, there was a rumpus in the hotel lounge and two *gendarmes* entered, supporting an elderly gentleman with a cane. Apparently, I had omitted to put on the hand brake; the car had drifted down the sloping street; knocking over this elderly inhabitant of Belley. Bernard led the three of them into the bar and plied them with whisky, so that the *gendarmes* failed to ask for any papers, which was just as well, as I had let the insurance ran out. We then collected this delicate regional fish which was so large that the *bain-marie* containing the

---

*Wartime retreat of Gertrude Stein, Alice B. Toklas and their tailor Pierre Balmain.

marinade stretched right across the rear seat and we had to drive back to Montaigre at forty kilometres an hour.

François was a very generous host and liked filling his house with people. In the evenings, he either entertained them conversationally, sitting cross-legged on his chair like a large, jovial baby squatting on its pot, or by thumping on the piano. I employ this term, for I always enjoy listening to Chopin, Schubert or Bach, but whenever François sat down at the piano, I had an immense urge to go to bed. The catering was done by a wily, dishonest Moroccan with a lively imagination, who not only might try and slip into your bed in the middle of the night, but, while the guests dined, would siphon the petrol out of their cars, leaving just enough for them to get home, so that the loss would not be noticed until the following day.

Chapter XVIII

Guests

After June Churchill, the next person to turn up out of the blue was Old Bill. By then the *mas* had been fully furnished with marble tables and swivelling armchairs, the kind one sees in luxury offices, only instead of turning to face a pavement, one had a glimpse of mountains.

One day a Simca came tearing up the hill and after backing into the mimosa that Joseph had just planted, Old Bill got out and came running across the terrace, carrying a Biot wine flask. He greeted me joyfully with, 'If you'd had this house when I first knew you, we'd have been married all these years!' Goodness, what I'd missed! Then he ran back to the car, and reappeared with a Rolleiflex and, careering down towards the vines, leaving crushed shoots in his wake, with parted legs, muscles bulging, the camera balanced on his paunch, he snapped and snapped away. But the results turned out to be overexposed. While we sat drinking on the terrace, he remarked on the olive tree in front of Bernard's quarters.

'Yes, don't knock it over. It's only just been planted,' I said.

'That size?'

'Yes, it cost me a packet.'

'It's good to hear you boasting', he complimented me, 'you never used to,' adding, 'You've stopped bleaching your hair, I see.' When Bernard went into the kitchen to replenish the *bidon* of wine, Bill said, 'He reminds me of that Hamilton boy. Only this one looks even younger. *Nice work if you can get it.*' And he went on humming down the scale . . . 'Doh ray me fa so lat te doh . . . What is it you like so much about Jews?'

'Noses,' I said.

The odd fact was that of all my friends, Bill was the one that Bernard got on with best. Did they have some affinity? *Hommes de menage!*

135

Appreciators of good food and wine. After scouring the hillside for herbs, Bill came running back with some dandelion shoots, wild thyme, fennel and lemon verbena and, while Bernard went on filling the *bidon*, he prepared a delicious *aioli*. They could have set up house together! Numerous marriages, countless girls and jobs, and just turning sixty, with no wife, girl or job, and on the look-out for all three, Bill went on humming down the scale until we all settled down to eat beneath the eucalyptus tree. He was staying with his ex, he said.

'Mind you, I was never in love with her. I might have been if she'd had better breasts. But she just didn't turn me on. Don't you miss people here?'

'I prefer birds to people these days,' I said emptying the bread basket for the white turtle doves at our feet. Then the sirens went and we saw the thin spiral of smoke rising from across the valley. The next day, we learnt that the *vieille* in the *librairie* had let a bonfire get out of control.

At six o'clock I said, 'Isn't it time we went?' The Mercedes was being repaired in a garage in Cannes and Bill was driving us in. When we reached the main road, we got caught up in a traffic jam . . . doh ray me fa so la te doh . . . and wham, the Simca struck the rear of a Citroën and an irate Frenchman leapt out screaming abuse. By then the traffic was on the move and, with a flash of white teeth, Bill sped ahead just as the Simca door swung off its hinges. Dear old blunderbuss. He certainly was affectionate. As we drove into the garage, he gave me an enormous hug and kiss on the lips. A mechanic produced some rope with which to reattach the door and Bill went off merrily shouting, 'There's no doubt, you're much nicer to animals than you ever were to people.' What had I ever done to him?

He turned up again three years later, bringing a new wife, a baby, a babysitter and a backlog of dirty washing that they proceeded to ram into the washing machine and then spread across the terrace to dry. They departed after a week, leaving their bedroom walls covered in red graffiti, as the baby had been playing with lipstick.

Edwina wrote inviting herself and then arrived with a scowling lover, an enormous dog and a two-year-old baby with a permanent grin. They also stayed a week and then made a get-away, barely saying goodbye, before Thérèse had discovered that the urine-drenched mattress had also been hacked with a penknife. I never had much luck with guests.

It was during the pea and bean season that Jane arrived from the States with flowing, bleached hair looking like a beautiful transvestite. In the mornings, she stood naked at her bedroom window playing a flute. In the afternoons, she got into the car, lowered the hood and went sightseeing. At dusk the car appeared, tearing up the hill, a swarm of bees in its wake. A cat lover, Jane was amused by the way Mell strayed across the terrace, as though the gravel scorched her paws, but what Jane enjoyed even more was the emergence at drinks time of an enormous toad that did a methodic tour of the rosemary hedge, gulping down moths and mosquitoes. There was no particular mishap during this visit, but, being in the throes of writing *Un Siècle Débordé*, it was Bernard who felt guilt for not having given her enough attention and, as she stepped into the car to be taken to the station, he bowed so low while kissing her hand that he grazed his head.

One sunny day, we drove to Antibes to see Graham Greene, who lived in a large modern block where you announced yourself by shouting into a grill. His flat had a lovely view of the sea and I remember him saying that he would never recover the amount he had paid for it, whereas these days it would be worth far more. After Graham had mixed several excellent Martinis, we walked across to his favourite restaurant and Bernard related how, as an adolescent, he had always dreamt of entering Chez Feliks. During lunch, Graham had a long conversation with the patron that, at the time, I thought rather impolite, complaining of the incessant barking of dogs at night and asking what could be done about it. But having lived many more years in France, I now understand Graham's obsession. No matter where you are, there is always a barking dog in the vicinity; '*Chien Méchant*' boards deface practically every village gate. The French must feel protected by this brute that is usually lamenting the absence of some master or mistress, and no matter how often one visits the local *gendarmerie* (in principle no animal should disturb the peace after ten pm) no amount of discussion will resolve the problem. We drank a lot of Marc. Then, in spite of Graham reiterating, 'But this is *my* party,' Bernard insisted on paying the bill. As we were leaving, I suggested to Graham that he come and stay.

'There's plenty of room,' I said. 'We have four bedrooms.' He must have thought I was boasting and in a subdued tone went on repeating, 'Four bedrooms!' as though someone had related a miracle.

Bernard and I bickered all the way back to Grimaud, and we never saw Graham again.

I was often lonely but never bored. When Joseph no longer had the time to tend the garden, a succession of good-for-nothings came and went. Joseph's mentally retarded brother, the shepherd's stepson, a sturdy youth, carried a transistor and came up wearing a straw hat with a dangling pink ribbon; he took afternoon siestas in the meadow and surreptitiously gathered boulders off the property to carry away and build himself a *cabanon*. Then an old Italian peasant came. Surveying the surrounding chaos, he muttered, '*Beaucoup de boulot ici.*' In winter, should I go on to the terrace dressed in an old marmot fur coat and gold evening shoes that I was trying to wear out, he'd mutter, '*Quelle putain!*' In the evenings, he went home with his pockets stuffed with maize that was stacked in the garage for the *poules* and once, when I called on him in Grimaud, his wife guiltlessly handed me a plate of polenta she had made from it.

In June, rotted trees had to be sawn down and the wood piled ready to burn the following winter. In July, the apricots ripened and Thérèse made apricot jam. August was the time for gathering peaches, nectarines and almonds which got shelled while sitting beneath the mulberry tree – a way of ekeing out the evening drink.

Every few years the cork trees had to be stripped, leaving the boles a smooth, burnt ochre. A Moroccan came up to do that. Before carting away the cork to sell, he hosed it well with water to increase its weight. In winter, he went home and turned up again in the spring to fill in the potholes. He moved with incredible grace on horny black feet and once during my absence, seeing Thérèse sweeping upstairs, he climbed up on to the bedroom terrace and offered her thirty francs for a quickie. She rejected him politely, saying, 'I have Joseph for that sort of thing.' Or so she told me.

The last Sunday in August was the opening of the *chasse*. As soon as one opened the shutters, there would be a blast of rifle fire and lone huntsmen with their dogs would toil up the hill; after chalking '*Et ta soeur?*' ('Up yours!') on the hoardings inscribed '*Propriéte Privé*' and '*Défense de Chasser*', they fired on anything that moved. Even the turtle doves had to be caged, as if one flew across the valley, it would suddenly plummet. Anything white, *chasseurs'* delight, one could say. In fact, there was nothing much left in the forest to kill apart from stone martens, ferrets, an occasional rabbit, or foxes that haunted the terrace at night, making an eerie sound like a baby's wail. In the initial years, there were a few wild boars. Joseph would show me where they had been rubbing their backs against the bark of a tree. Then one day, he came up very excited to show me one he had shot, crammed into the boot of his car.

'*Regarde! Regarde!*' he kept saying. '*Comme il est beau!*' Just like the weather. The following day, there it was dangling by its feet outside the butcher's shop.

When his sons reached an age to handle a rifle, they would sneak up at dawn, park their car in the lane and, after gathering any *cèpes* they could find, creep, *à pied de loup*, on to the terrace to take pot-shots at the blackbirds in the olive tree. A blackbird's song is a lovely sound. I would tear out in a dressing gown, screaming abuse.

Joseph also liked laying traps for birds. He put them so close to the house that the cats would bring them in and lay them on the kitchen tiles, as much as to say, 'Look what I've found.' Joseph and his two sons were savages when it came to killing. Still, so was the writer, Isaak Dinesen, according to her book, *Out of Africa*:

Out of one hundred cartridges yesterday, I shot forty-four head of game, put a bullet right in the hearts of a wildebeest and a duiker. I shot twenty different kinds of game, all the ordinary specimens of deer, zebra, wildebeest, marabou, jackal, wild boar, one lion, one leopard and a number of large birds . . .

On early autumn mornings, the meadow would be moist with dew, cicadas chanted away and in the evenings mosquitoes haunted the terrace. Towards the end of this idyllic period, there was so much rain in the Midi that mushrooms grew rampantly. As well as *cèpes* that sprouted at the base of the oaks, there were *chanterelles*, little yellow flutes embedded in moist, dark soil, and the last to appear were the pink mushrooms that sprouted at the base of the umbrella pines. During the *vendange*, there would be singing in the valley. For the *vendange* was a *fête*. Open trucks piled high with glistening grapes trundled along the main road on their way to the Vinicole Co-Opérative and the whole countryside was permeated with a rank, sour smell. Driving into Grimaud, in the open car, I would pass Joseph standing like Ben Hur at the wheel of his truck, and he'd shout, '*Ça va? Ça va?*' and I would shout back, '*Oui. Ça va.*' The *vendange* over, the vine leaves turned russet red and large vans with Bavarian number plates would be parked outside the Vinicole Co-Op, their cisterns marked 'Beaujolais', when in fact they were being replenished with Côtes de Provence. More and more of the surrounding land became planted with vineyards, and now the Côtes de Provence wine is considered by some to be just as good as any ordinary Bordeaux.

Sometimes in autumn, I drove to the small sickle-shaped beach at Beauvallon. Swimming there was particularly agreeable after a *mistral*, with the sea brisk and chill, swept clear of floating pine stalks. Small yachts would be moored offshore, their sails billowing down in slats. I might have been invisible for all the attention I aroused in my old Twenties-style bathing outfit, and if by chance some monster's gaze happened to hover my way, it was only to settle on some plump young *Fräulein*, a left-over from the tourist season, lying close by on the sand. Sometimes, one saw the two *putes* who went there not to swim, but sunbathe, a pig-tailed blonde with full, white breasts, while the brunette's were small and *piquant*, and passing men would turn and smile, even if their wives were with them. At midday, everyone rose, and what bliss it was to be left alone with one's ugly thoughts of how old and despicable one was compared with Sagan, Eileen Geist or Bette, then Bernard's current lady in Paris.

Bored with the beach, I'd walk barefoot to the car, happy to note that one's hair had bleached a little, even if with the aid of Johnson's baby oil, though the poor old skin refused to golden as before.

Back at home, the table laid beneath the eucalyptus — *pain de campagne* . . . butter . . . a hunk of *gruyère* . . . tomatoes out of the garden. I might open a bottle of Perrier Jouet Rosé 1964 and how delicious it tasted drinking it alone.

Chapter XIX

In the Pink

Just before I married Derek, Aunty Greta wrote to say Mummy had asked her to send me a note to tell me she was not very well and she thought I ought to know she had very high blood pressure. The doctor had told her, Aunty Greta added, that Mummy had had a slight stroke. She was in bed, and had to be kept very quiet and must rest. Aunty Greta had let Brenda know, but Mummy had asked her to tell me not to worry.

'We are hoping she will be up and about again soon, and we all send our love.'

Two years later, while staying in Claridge's, I drove down to my aunt's house on Hythe seafront. Mummy occupied the upstairs sittingroom and had a view of the sea from her bed and her own upstairs bathroom. She could move about but she never went down to meals. I can't remember what I took – probably gin, for that is what the aunts liked to drink. Mummy was not exactly hale and hearty, but it never entered my head that she was seriously ill. A year later, when I was in the Midi, I got a telegram saying, 'Mummy gravely ill'. I went into Grimaud to telephone. Aunty Hilda answered and said, 'Mummy wants to see you.' She was in a nursing home. I was in great pain myself, at the time. In fact, soon after, I entered the American hospital in Paris. When I left for England, although his sister was arriving the following day, Bernard accompanied me into St Raphael, where we drank several Martinis in a hotel opposite the station. I parked the car in a garage and Bernard took a taxi home. When I got into the sleeper I took a Tuinal and was still sleeping when the Blue Train drew into the Gare de Lyon. In the train to Calais, the *douanier* entered the compartment and confiscated 400 francs – then you were not allowed to take out more than 200. When I got on to the ferry I sent Eileen a telegram asking her to arrange an appointment with a gynaecologist. And from Dover I took a taxi. The following day, I went to see Mummy. The nursing home had once been a private house. Rose bushes bloomed in the garden that looked on to the canal bank, where couples sat sunning. It was Sunday, and church bells chimed as the nurse opened the door and led the way to Mummy's room. Bending over the bed, she lugged Mummy's inert form upright, saying, 'Now then, Mrs Skelton, your daughter from Mars is here.' The response was a plaintive grunt. 'She's been so looking forward to your coming. She's a dear little patient, gives us no trouble at all.' The praise would have pleased Mummy, for that is how she had always thought of herself, 'a dear little thing'. But how could she give trouble! Poor Mummy. There she lay, paralysed down the whole of one side of her body.

'Is she in pain?'

'She suffers from bed sores, but we're keeping her under sedation.'

Already anxious to make a get-away, I said, 'Isn't it a pity to wake her?' But at that moment Mummy opened her eyes and gave a crooked smile.

'That's a good girl,' said the nurse. 'I'll leave you now. Ring if you should need me. She likes having her forehead dabbed with eau-de-Cologne.'

Although paralysed, Mummy could still move one arm; her face was lopsided, she could hear what one said, but had great difficulty in making herself understood and talked huskily. They had taken away her teeth and her mouth had caved in. She was being spoonfed on slops and jellies. There was a certain dignity about her paralysed state. One arm rested above the bedclothes, the paralysed arm lay beneath the sheet.

'How thin you are, Barbara,' she said hoarsely.

'Every time you've seen me in the last few years, you've said that,' I told her. She gave a crooked smile and went on croaking what I interpreted as 'heir', referring to her will, which only shows how the subconscious works when someone is dying; eventually I realised she meant 'hair', as she was used to seeing it bleached. I remarked on how marvellous her skin looked. She had so few wrinkles, though her neck sagged a little.

'Michael Arlen always said I had marvellous skin,' she lisped. Then her eyes closed and she began to fade. I was about to leave when Brenda entered the room with the matron and between them they kept up a conversation about Mummy as though she were already dead, and I saw her looking at them with pleading, desperate eyes. Dying people's eyes become very expressive, betraying any fear or anguish. Mummy had asked me to see her doctor, which I did the following day. I don't know what she expected from the visit, perhaps to be told something encouraging. The doctor said she had cancer of the lungs, but as she was eighty-three it would not be advisable to operate. She was not in pain or being given any drugs. Her heart was sound and she had a lot of resistance. Mummy had also asked to be brought her handbag, which I took to her the following day. The aunts had removed all her money, justifying it by saying, 'You never know in a nursing home!' Mummy was very pleased to have her handbag. I asked what it was she wanted. Money? Oh no! Only her *powderpuff*, and there and then, with her one operative limb, her left hand, she delved into it and dabbed and dabbed away at her contorted face. Then her eyes closed and she began to weaken. I went round every day. One never knew what to say. I would smooth her brow with eau-de-Cologne, until she became increasingly irascible, as though her nerves were on edge. We took her flowers – in pots, hoping they would last out until the end.

Brenda was worried. What to do if Mummy lingered on and on? The nursing home was costing £40 a week.

'Brenda's such a worrier,' Aunty Greta kept complaining, and the aunts became increasingly irritated by Brenda's dog that whined nonstop whenever Brenda left the house. The one time I walked to the nursing home with Brenda and her dog, it was drizzling, and the dog never stopped tripping us up and tugging at its leash. One afternoon, I was alone with Mummy and I heard her say, 'I know now. I shall never be well again.' She realised she was going to die, but it didn't seem to worry her. June 25 was her birthday. Brenda had gone home. All the aunts, Vera, Greta and Hilda, took Mummy a present. I had bought her a rose chiffon nightdress. Mummy was lying propped up, wearing her new nightie, her lopsided face resting against the pillow.

'How are you feeling, Evie?' Aunty Vera said, in her usual bright manner.

'In the pink, thank you,' Mummy intoned. It was her *dernier bon mot*.

Two days later, Aunty Greta cooked us a roast. That evening, we were all seated round the gateleg table in the sittingroom eating, when the telephone rang. Aunty Greta answered. It was the matron. She asked to speak to me.

'Your mother passed away an hour ago. Would you come round as soon as possible and collect her things?'

The aunts murmured, 'Poor Evie!' 'It's all for the best.' Then, with bent heads, we all went on silently wolfing the dinner.

Mummy was buried beside Daddy in the pretty Saltwood church cemetery. No one cried at the funeral. Aunty Hilda seemed to be the most upset; she threw rose petals on to the grave. Then Brenda and I set off in a taxi to London, where I took a train back to Mars.

In Dunkirk, the tugmen were on strike, so I went back via Calais. In Paris, I went to an oculist and ordered more reading glasses. The gynaecologist said I had an ovarian cyst and made an appointment for me to see a surgeon. I lunched with Eileen. Then Bernard telephoned to know when I would be back.

'Tomorrow,' I said, 'or maybe the day after.'

When I got to St Raphael, the car refused to start and broke down twice on the way back. It was very hot. When I got to the *mas*, there was no sign of Bernard, the front door was ajar and the stereo had been left on the repeat. So I locked up and drove on to Garde-Freinet to stay with Pippa and Peter Forster. The next day, driving back to Grimaud, the car broke down again.

Bernard was sitting beside his suitcases on the terrace. He had spent the last days carousing with Sagan in St Tropez. I thought to myself, *and in these circumstances*. (I had been booked into the American hospital two weeks from then.)

'You don't want me to leave, do you?' he said, and, after my initial ill humour, we made up.

The *mas* had been rented to Americans for August. There were a lot of things to do. The following day I went into St Tropez to change a cheque. Bernard came with me. He had to see Sagan, he said, to fix up an abode while I was in the hospital. He was very helpful during the shopping. On the port he saw a blonde in a purple outfit and said, *'Comme elle est chic.'* I was in pain, uncombed and shabby. I thought, *merde*, all my money goes on having to support *two* people.

'Why are you in a bad humour? Oh, to be free,' he sighed. I left him in Senequiers and went off to buy a pair of shoes. Passing Senequiers again and seeing him sitting with Sagan's husband, Bob Westoff, I say, *'Maintenant, vous êtes libre,'* giving a curt upward gesture of the hand, as much as to say, 'Hi' and 'goodbye'. Feeling lonely and dejected, I walked on lugging a basket of *dorade*, new shoes and with my handbag strapped over one shoulder. I had just reached Félix Potin the grocers when he caught me up.

'It is only 11.30 and Françoise is still asleep. I'll leave a message. Come and have a drink,' he said.

'No thank you.'

'Well, don't be cross. Do you feel bad?' He kissed me and went off.

I returned to the house. It rained and rained. I felt so sad. At 3.30 a telegram arrived, despatched from Sainte Maxime: *'Je déjeune. J'arrive. Tendresse. Bernard.'* A man came to repair the fridge. At 4.30 I decided to go back and change the shoes I had bought that morning. St Tropez was more packed then ever. I bought tomatoes for the *dorade*, did not change the shoes and got home at 5.30, only to find all the shutters closed and the front door locked. I had not taken a key. Frantic, I drove off to the locksmith in Cogolin. He came up with a jemmy, but then said he needed help. So, I went across to Thérèse who accompanied me back. Thérèse was always very reassuring on occasions like this. She listened at the bathroom window.

'Monsieur Bernard! It's Térèse! He's in there, I hear snoring,' she said to me, rapping on the shutter. After some time, he opened up, so drunk he could hardly walk. He explained to Thérèse that the shutters had been closed because of the rain.

It was always like that whenever Sagan came to St Tropez. That evening, Sagan came to fetch him. She did not drive up, but remained at the bottom of the hill and hooted, and Bernard walked down carrying his suitcases.

Whenever he was in Normandy, Cahors or Paris, he wired or wrote regularly, sometimes twice a week: '*Tu me manques déjà à bientôt j'espère t'embrasse très fort.*'

When in Normandy, '*J'ai tout de même trouvé moyen d'aller au casino pour jouer à blackjack, jeu difficile car les cartes vont très vite. Hier pour raison de régime une coupe de champagne orange au Royal et pendant le dîner le tiers d'une bouteille de Bordeaux . . . mes essais de travailler me donnent des soucis . . .*'

One day a telegram arrived saying, '*Le coati nomme Bernard arrive à Nice*', and off went the squaw to the airport.

When the first forest fire broke out round Garde-Freinet, we were in the throes of having the telephone installed and a man had come up to supervise the placing of the poles.

'No poles near the house,' I shouted down from the bedroom window, 'I don't want to hamper the view.' Later, when a team of men were digging at the bottom of the hill for the wires to pass through and I complained of a branch being lopped off, an official came running up and, after scanning me from every angle, as much as to say 'nothing doing', snapped, 'Well, Madame, do you want to have the telephone installed here or not?'

All day, planes had been flying backwards and forwards to St Raphael to fill up with seawater to quench the flames, and it never entered our heads that we were in any danger until late in the afternoon, when Bernard was crossing the terrace carrying a lightly boiled egg, like a participant in an egg and spoon race, we heard a sudden hiss of sizzling *maquis* and, looking up, saw the whole of the adjoining hillock in flames, whereupon the telephone official joined us. Surveying the oncoming devastation, he turned and said, 'Well, Madame, it doesn't look as though you'll be needing the telephone, after all,' got into his car and drove swiftly down the hill. We were debating what to do when a Deux Chevaux drove up. Thérèse and her daughter got out and shouted, 'You must leave at once.' The two of them then gathered up all the garden paraphernalia and carried it into the house, and closed all the shutters while we packed. They drove away warning us not to dally, but should we get trapped by smoke to make for a vineyard, as being cleared of debris, it was the only safe place. Indeed, when the fire eventually abated and stretches of forest were reduced to black charred stumps, the only undevastated areas were the vineyards.

It is quite difficult to decide what to pack in a hurry. I took a toothbrush, reading glasses, a dressing gown and a book, but forgot to include an overcoat. It was late October, a *mistral* raged and the car was open. The animals piled into the back, we drove away. All the valley dwellers had departed early that morning, their cars stacked with bedding. When we reached Grimaud, I remember getting out of the car and looking back at the smoke screening the valley with tears pouring down my face, like Scarlett when fleeing Tara, while Bernard murmured, 'Is the house insured?' Then we joined a stream of cars heading for Toulon, stopping every so often at a café to warm up on Cognac. In Toulon, most of the hotels were full. We eventually found a double room. Bernard had no trouble getting to sleep, but I spent most of the night fretting.

When the *mistral* had abated, we drove back to find four members of the fire brigade installed, with sleeping bags, in the garage and a fire engine in the drive. They remained on the terrace for days, which made one feel protected. I would take them cups of coffee and drive into Grimaud to get their bread. At nights, should a faint breeze revive the smouldering tree stumps, the men would make a systematic tour of the forest quenching any flickering flames that, from my bedroom window, looked like myriad glow-worms. The smell of burnt bracken lingered on for weeks.

My first summer in Grimaud, Cyril came to stay, bringing a paperback of *The Unquiet Grave* – 'With love from Cyril, London 1967. Two corks that have been over Niagara. Bobbing along in the shallows.' As I was alone, not wishing to be compromised, he booked a room in a Sainte Maxime hotel. At that time, Deirdre assumed me to be a witch. When Cressida was born, I had not been allowed to see her, as it was feared I would give the baby the evil eye.

The next time Cyril came to Grimaud, he was on his way home from Kenya and had spent the night on the plane. He arrived so tired that he immediately went up to bed and fell asleep. I did not want to wake him, but Bernard thought he would not want to miss dinner. I cannot recall the menu, but I do remember that during the dessert course, a pot of cream aimed at me skimmed past Cyril's head, as I was listening too intently to his observations on Proust and Diderot, and an Englishman was not considered to be sufficiently knowledgeable about either. But Cyril certainly knew the meaning of *'vieux gâteux'* and, the following morning, when I took him his breakfast, he was already planning a get-away. He only looked up from the array of timetables spread across the bed to say, 'I pity you, Barbara. Your priorities are all wrong. You've let this man abolish all your powers of action. Get out before it's too late. Either it's real love of a sado-masochistic kind, or you are just frittering your life away on a futile, neurotic situation, cutting yourself off from all other sources of pleasure, intellectual activities, friendships, travel. Buy yourself some pretty clothes, for God's sake.' Intellectual activities! There was no time for that sort of thing any more, all my energy being expended on running a large house, choosing tiles for the construction of a swimming pool, deciding whether or not to have the shutters repainted or buying new material for the wine-drenched cushions. There was a plane strike on at the time and what, in fact, Cyril wanted me to do was to drive him up to Paris. He said he liked Bernard, adding that I did not take him seriously enough as a writer, as Joan (with whom he identified me at the time) did Paddy Leigh Fermor. For both men were very alike . . . talented, irascible writers, appreciators of good food and wine, animal lovers, with a coterie of admiring women and a *penchant* for disorderly, book-infested dens. When Cyril had gone, I teased Bernard by saying, 'You ought to have more respect for a man so much older than yourself! At any rate, Cyril earns a living, has the courage to support a family and still has immense curiosity about everything. Whereas, all *you* have any curiosity about is trying out some brand of catfood for Suki or Mell!'

Who, then, would have foretold that fifteen years later, Bernard would also be a *paterfamilias*, supporting a charming wife and two delightful *petites filles*?

Cyril and I went on keeping in touch. I used to feel quite lost if weeks went by without getting a letter from him containing snaps of Cressida and his son, Matthew, on the back of which he wrote 'From your old baby'. But our meetings in London were never a great success. He became increasingly bored listening to my woes and would suddenly announce he had a train to catch. We would bustle off to Victoria and, sometimes, I would accompany him as far as Lewes, and take the next train back.

What is sad, once a loving relationship is severed, is that there is nothing much left to say. Meals with Cyril became reminiscent of those we used to take with his mother when she came over from South Africa and her 'darling sprat' barely looked up from his plate.

On another of Cyril's visits to the *mas*, he seemed to have come in order to probe through a hoard of old letters and he spent most of his time on his knees before a large wicker basket in my bedroom, so dead set on what he was doing that he even refused to come down to one meal. After rummaging through the lot, his only comment was, 'You certainly were a sexpot in your day,' and even to this day, I don't know what he took.

The very last visit was after he had had an operation for a cataract. He arrived in September to spend his birthday with us, bringing a long-standing *admiratrice*, Shelagh Levita, the calm mother that he had always claimed he needed. Shelagh had long, sleek, dark hair, and a certain chic; she dressed in simple, well-cut, tailored suits. She was someone you could count on, self-sacrificing and kind. The only thing she lacked, from my point of view, was a sense of humour.

On the morning of his birthday, Cyril sat out on the terrace with his back to the sun to protect his eyes. He was taking us both out to lunch; Bernard had declined. In fact, as Cyril sat studying the *Michelin*, an open car shot up the hill with the radio at full blast, and a scrupulously dressed Bernard strolled across the terrace, got into it and disappeared for the rest of the day.

At one o'clock I went into Cyril's room to see if he were ready, to find him fully dressed with his hat on, seated on the edge of the bed, bent over in pain.

'Are you sure you wouldn't like me to call a doctor?' I said.

To my surprise, he said, 'Yes, I would. I know what happens to people in my condition, they choke to death.'

The only intimation I had had of his being at all ill was earlier that year when he wrote to say he had been quite unwell due to some heart trouble, 'which is now under control, but my pills may not work if I do too much or get more infection; my second-hand valve is clearly deteriorating, mileage very heavy – but no high blood pressure, no warnings not to eat or climb stairs etc., only to avoid going out into the cold after a meal.' Then I remembered that the previous summer, when he and Shelagh had come to stay, after swimming in the pool, he had had great difficulty climbing out and complained of a terrible pain in his chest, blaming it on the absence of steps leading out of the swimming pool.

There was a very good heart specialist attached to the hospital in St Tropez, a Doctor Couve, who became the Mayor. His assistant came up immediately. Alas, there was no birthday lunch and the following day I drove Cyril into hospital to be operated on. The telephone was ringing when I got home. It was François Michel who had it in mind to come and stay. When told that Couve planned to operate to remove the liquid around Cyril's heart, François immediately exclaimed, 'Don't let them. That operation always proves fatal.'

After the operation, I asked Couve's assistant what chance Cyril had of getting well and he employed a depressing analogy. His condition, he said, could be compared to that of an old car that needed to have all its spare parts renewed. That evening, I telephoned Deirdre. Shouldn't she fly out? But she had no intention of doing that.

The hospital did not have a very good reputation. The equipment was dated, the rooms were like prison cells. The nurses gave the impression that tanning was their main motive in being there. Bernard telephoned his cardiologist in Paris, who recommended a hospital in Cannes. Cyril was happy to leave St Tropez. He refused to be taken out on a stretcher. He dressed himself, put on his Homburg and walked down the hospital steps to the ambulance. Shelagh was with me and said, 'Do you think I should go with him?' And although I felt so sad and would have preferred her to remain, we agreed it was the best thing to do and she got into the ambulance. I was never to see Cyril dressed and on his feet again and for months afterwards, every time I saw the back of an ambulance, I relived the scene. That evening, I went into Cannes to pick up Shelagh and we drove back along the autoroute almost blinded by a thick sea mist.

147

As Bernard and I slept at opposite ends of the house, and his quarters were next to the kitchen, contact was often made by notes being left in the sink. The following day, I read:

Barbara. I would appreciate it if you and Shyla [sic] could control as much as possible your visits to the kitchen so that I can work a little. It is much less tiring for me to clear up the dishes left in the sink than to hear your sudden and incessant comings and goings. The noise of the dishwasher, because it is monotonous and regular, doesn't disturb me as much. As for knowing whether or not that's costing us a lot in electricity, I think you have dealt with the question by allowing the heating to be on practically all day. What's more, as you know (because I've told you so many times) your steps, your manner of walking is abrupt.

Of course this doesn't mean you can't go into the kitchen. All I'm asking is for a little good will . . .

Soon after, Shelagh moved into a hotel in Cannes to be close to the hospital. Cyril complained of the food and asked me to take him some *oeufs en gêlée*. The heart specialist there was optimistic about Cyril's future and, in time, he was well enough to board a plane and, right up to the moment of his departure, he kept planning to take Shelagh and me to a final lunch in a star restaurant.

Back in London he telephoned; his voice sounded very faint and would suddenly fade away altogether, as though the receiver had dropped out of his hand. Two weeks later, he was in the Harley Street Clinic and Shelagh wrote to say she had delayed writing to thank me for having her to stay so that she could give me news about Cyril, adding that I had made her feel very welcome long after she should have left:

I am most grateful, as staying in hotels is awful alone. Cyril still eats nothing, though I think the food is good and a large menu. He is still very weak and finds walking from the bed to the bathroom very tiring. In the last two days, the breathlessness has come back at nights. On the other hand, they are giving him cardiograms or X-rays and taking blood pressure only twice a day, so one imagines they are not worried. He is seeing a heart specialist this Wednesday. They say breathlessness is from excess fluid in the stomach. Possibly the weakness is simply because he does not eat. You and Bernard did so much for him. Hope to see you here again soon . . .

The next letter said that Cyril had seen a top London heart specialist, Lawson-McDonald, who had given him an optimistic report. He told Cyril he must stay a further month in the clinic, having injections of vitamins and diuretics, and at the end of that time, he would be and feel better. Doctor Goldman had seen him that morning and said they had been worried when he first went into the nursing home because he could not lose enough fluid, but he also believed that he had turned the corner and would improve.

He is going to give Cyril the injections himself so that they are less painful. All in all, good news. C. sends a message that he would like you to get him some mangosteens [an exotic fruit] from Fauchon in the Place de la Madeleine to give to Andrew Devonshire in the hope that he may be able to grow plants from seed . . .

And she looked forward to seeing me the following week.

Chapter XX

Cyril's Death

When I visited the Harley Street Clinic, the first thing that struck me was the dust and the array of dead flowers cluttering the room. Why had no one bothered to throw them away? My visits could not coincide with Deirdre, Sonia, Joan or Janetta's. But Shelagh was always there until my last visit, when C. was alone. He was studying a medical encyclopaedia, when two doctors entered. They were doing their rounds. Cyril addressed them querulously:

'Why is it I'm not getting any better?' The doctors seemed to be baffled as to what was the actual cause of his illness. Was it a heart or a liver complaint?

'Have you ever lived in the tropics?' one of them said.

Cyril was pitifully thin. He lacked appetite, but could be persuaded to drink a little glucose. If I sat too far away from the bed, a pained expression clouded his face. His vision was impaired. Although in exasperated moments he had often compared Ann Fleming to 'an old French letter in a telephone booth' he was hurt that neither she nor John Betjeman had been to see him. He said, 'Nature's become hostile.' Then, maybe to test me out, he said he hoped to live another five years.

'Please, Cyril, don't talk like that,' I said.

'But five years is a long time,' he replied, and proceeded to tell me how he would like to spend them. I left the clinic crying and soon after returned to Grimaud. Once more alone.

Shelagh's last letter said that Cyril had been transferred to King's College Hospital where they specialised in liver diseases, but she gathered they were more concerned about his heart condition and that this had to be improved before turning to the liver, but she wished they would keep him on there, as they had a most competent team who were doing all they could and he was being fed intravenously.

One rainy November day, soon after, Shelagh telephoned to say that Cyril had died that morning. She had been with him right up to the last moment.

Then an odd thing happened. The days following his death, whenever I came back from shopping, though I had had no recollection of having touched the switch, the light bulb on the small terrace leading off my upstairs bedroom would be lit. It had never happened before and it was never to happen again. I like to interpret it as having been a signal of farewell.

I drove to Normandy, where Bernard was staying with Sagan in her manor house, not far from Honfleur. On the first evening I was talking to the secretary, Isabelle, who said, 'What have you been doing lately? I hear you've been communing with the dead.' She thought it a huge joke. I must have been in a good humour, for Isabelle and I laughed so much that the film producer, Roger Vadim, who was talking to Françoise, turned to me and said, 'May I ask where you come from?' – a question the French often pose, meaning, where are your roots?

'Maidenhead,' I said.

As Sagan had a full house (or should I say manor?), although her brother politely asked me to stay on, I drove to Seine-et-Marne for the New Year and spent it with François Michel.

Previous Convictions is dedicated to 'B.S.'

'Oak before ash, look out
        for a splash'
With love as always to Barbara.
Too bad I could not find an elm anywhere!
It is also dedicated to you in the last sentence.
December 1963.

I have left out one phenomenon besides the search for truth and the obsession with the form and shaping of a work of art – the devotion which is distilled, after years, from all the possessive kinds of love; which may have originated in boredom, unhappiness, habit, or lust, from an accident of fusion that creates something profound and selfless ('the giving which plays us least false') like the love of parents for a child which yet keeps something of the child about it – a positive, permanent illusion, a projection of lost early loves on to one person. In the field of discovery and the world of love miracles still happen. The presence of one of these long-suffering ac-complices in our last act of existence may help to ease us out of it, or, when all those whom we have truly loved are dead, they may suffice to tip the scales for death, until dying becomes a renewal of communication with them. The rest is mineral emptiness.

It was during his last illness that Cyril arranged for me to meet his daughter, Cressida. As she seemed prepared to brave my evil eye, we met for lunch in Knightsbridge, where Cressida ordered steak and chips with a green salad. We got on well and have been seeing each other ever since. The following summer she came to Grimaud. Gerda was also staying on a short visit from the States and, although previously Bernard had never spent July or August in the Midi, for he dreaded the heat, he also turned up. It was an extremely hot summer. Gerda and Cressida spent their days basking beside the swimming pool. I was not at my best dealing with such diverse people, one of whom could not communicate in English. In the evenings, garrulous Gerda and I sat beneath the mulberry tree peeling and salting almonds that we had gathered to accompany our drinks. One evening, Bernard joined us. He was knowledge-ably holding forth on Anglo-Saxon authors, when I jubilantly announced, French style, '*à table*' and we all moved across to the café table where four roast quails were waiting. Cressida apparently did not care for small birds with legs like twigs unless they were overcooked. As Bernard had bought the quails, he got angry and accused her of being '*mal élevée*'; she began to cry and ran upstairs to her room. The following night, we had *rougets* for dinner and when Cressida raised her fork to sniff the fish to see if it were fresh, Bernard again angrily accused her of being spoilt and ill-mannered, and ordered her to leave the table; once again, she ran up to her room sobbing. I went up to console her, when we heard a crash.

'Something's been flung on to the tiles,' she said.

'Don't worry, I'm used to that,' I assured her.

Finally, everyone calmed down and the four of us were once more seated at the table, when, to this day – the reason remains a mystery – Bernard rose slowly to his feet holding a carafe of wine and emptied it over my head. Stunned, I just sat there, with wine pouring down my neck and Gerda couldn't stop laughing. Cressida ran upstairs for the last time, locked herself into her room and did not reappear until the following day when, curtailing their visit, the ladies packed their bags and were driven to the airport.

When the property the other side of the valley was put up for sale and the farmhouse had become uninhabitable, the Delmassos moved to the outskirts of Grimaud. Thérèse still went on coming to clean, riding up on a *mobylette*. Then, when the financial squeeze set in and nearly every villa on the coast had a 'For Sale' sign up, as I couldn't afford to have her more than twice a week, she never abandoned me altogether but went to work full time for a hotel in St Tropez and came to me on her day off, when she could.

One day, a bulldozer was seen ploughing up the track opposite the farmhouse, which was demolished, and in place of a copse of cork oaks one had a view of a new large house and what turned out to be a gleaming swimming pool.

Soon after, in spite of everyone saying that it was only fit for *sangliers*, a piece of land adjoining mine was bought by the Marquis de Mirepoix, a charming gentleman whose family dated back to the tenth century.* Once again a bulldozer appeared. This time it shoved its way up the adjoining hill and the Marquis came to offer me a strip of land which had some very fine old trees (when I had too many trees already) in return for a strip of my land on the hill just behind the *mas*, the site he had chosen for his future villa. We would have been at shouting distance. When I declined his offer, his little wife came to charm me, for she too had been a *mannequin* and we were certain to come to an agreement. When I still refused to give in, the Marquis surprised me by saying, 'In that case, you will not be invited to our housewarming.' It did not deter him from dropping in on us later whenever his telephone was out of order.

It took over a year for the construction of his house and the din was infernal. Then during the levelling of the ground for the layout of a garden, the bulldozer blocked the *ruisseau* that channelled the heavy rain into the valley in winter; the *ruisseau* changed course and torrents of rain swept past my terrace. The Mirepoix were in Paris, I had to consult a lawyer. By this time, everyone in the valley considered the new residents to be a couple of crashing bores and all romantic association with the area had vanished. For once the Mirepoix were installed in their pink, stucco villa, instead of the sound of birds when the shutters were opened, one would hear shouts, the hum of a mowing machine or belly-flops, for they too had built a swimming pool.

The *mas* was put into the hands of an estate agent. Alas, one had missed the boom period. Interested buyers could not afford the price and the house remained on sale for another two years, when a European arms millionaire made a reasonable offer.

The year the *mas* was sold, there happened to have been a property scandal in the area. A villa had been bought illegally by one of Giscard's ministers. Soon after, the minister was found dead in a *marais* outside Paris and, to this day, it is not known whether his death was suicide or murder. My *notaire* had negotiated the sale. This put everyone in a tizzy, for the *mas* was being sold as it had been bought, the sum above the declared price being paid under the table.

---

* In the eighteenth century, there was a bishop of Mirepoix who liked to sign himself '*anc*' (*ancien*); Voltaire pretended to read it as *âne*, so that his enemy, the bishop, forever after became known as the Mitred Ass or the Donkey of Mirepoix.

The day the deal was to go through, the buyer and I met in the estate agent's office, and there we all had the sticky task of counting out several thousand, freshly minted franc notes. It was nearing mid-day when we all walked across to the *notaire* and only when I had finished signing away the *mas* did the agent hand me the wad under the *notaire*'s table.

I remained in the *mas* for another three months. The very last visitor was Old Bill, who arrived with a present of some leftovers out of his fridge. He had just been through another divorce and was having a 'walkout', he said, with an actor's wife, having seduced her in a sandpit opposite his house. I knew of this pit. It was where, when I went to stay with him in the Sarthe, Suki and the village cats did biggies and pee pee, and it struck me as odd that anyone should find it an ideal seduction site.

Old B. stated he was on his way to Corsica to visit a widower whom he had known for thirty years.

'Poor old chap. Buried alive on that island.' They were going to have a nostalgic get-together to bemoan the fact that at their age it was no longer so easy to find a well-endowed young wife. Corsica. That old flame of mine. Might I come too? So Old B. wrote and arranged for me to go with him.

Some days before our departure, he kept running on to the terrace dragging a length of string. Finally, I became curious.

'Whatever are you doing?'

'It's in your interest,' he said, and darted out again. Coming back, he stated, 'Your car being two inches shorter than mine, we'll go in yours. It'll be cheaper on the ferry.'

Come D-Day, late in the evening, I put little Suki and her basket on to the back seat of the car. Old B. said irritably, 'Can't you leave that cat on the terrace? She can fend for herself.'

We arrived in Nice with time to kill.

'We'll go into a café and order a sandwich,' said Old B. Sit over a sandwich for a couple of hours? No siree! I drove into the old quarter, where the flower market was held, and we found a small restaurant with a menu at fifty francs each: fish soup, grilled sardines with sauté potatoes, cheese, bread and fruit, and a carafe of vino. While Old B. was working out to the last sou each one's share of the bill, I said, 'I've had such a tiring day. Would you mind driving the Datsun on to the ferry?'

'I'm not your chauffeur,' was the response. We argued all the way to the *quai*, and can Old B. get flushed and snappy, when he's not getting his own way.

We arrived on the jetty and I said, 'I think it's best if you go over without me.' He hauled his suitcase out of the boot and with it a blanket, for he planned to sleep like a down-and-out in a gangway and I set off home. He telephoned early next morning, while I was drinking coffee on the terrace.

Was his car all right? Why, did he fear that I had pushed it over the brink of a hill? He was returning in a couple of days, he said. He arrived with a present of a tiny bottle of crude alcohol that his host had given him.

A few weeks later, I wrote to Old B.'s friend and suggested I visit him on my own. An exchange of letters followed. He wrote to say he would meet me on the *quai* of Ajaccio. I drove into Nice at dawn, to find a queue of people waiting to buy car tickets and the ferry jam full. Passengers were pressed like sardines against the rails. Three quarters of an hour later, I walked out of the *bureau* with my car ticket to see the ferry part from the jetty and sail majestically out to sea. Back in the *bureau*, the man said, 'There's another ferry leaving from Marseille this afternoon. If you hurry, you might catch it.' I drove straight back to the *mas*, stopping on the way to send a telegram that reached Ajaccio two days later.

Still being in possession of a ticket to Ajaccio, I wrote again, inviting myself. Third time lucky. I took the plane to Ajaccio and there was Tim standing at the luggage belt behind a trolley that he had thoughtfully procured for my baggage. Uneffusive, passive and polite, my mother would surely have classified him as being 'the perfect gentleman'. He never stopped opening doors.

'After you.' 'No, after you.'

Is not excessive *politesse* slightly suspect? A camouflage? A way of keeping your distance? Whatever. Give me a more direct approach. Why the hell have you come? What a bore it's been having to meet you at the airport. Tim drove silently to his house where we were greeted by a huge, woolly-haired dog, a monster on hind legs.

'Down! Down! Rachmaninov, *down!*' Suki had to be hidden.

The house was *style* Charles Addams. On one corner was a circular tower like a castle on a chessboard. French windows looked on to an unattended garden. Plumbago grew rampant. There were citrus trees with large, crinkly marmalade oranges. Tim lived three flights up on the top floor with a lovely view of the harbour, partly hidden by towering blocks of flats, their terraces strewn with washing, men's shirts being strung up by their cuffs. Tim lived simply: no television; only a little radio to listen to jingle-jingle music. From his dining area, one saw fishing smacks scudding across the water. In the evenings, strains of Tino Rossi drifted our way. Lights flickered and the reddening sky was a picture. Tim prepared nice meals: napkins; a *couvert*; Danish sprats *fumées* and packaged in Germany; packaged Italian ham sliced thinly; crabmeat, fancy grade, produce of Thailand, Rotterdam merchandising; boxed Caprice de Dieu cheese. The only indigenous food were tomatoes and lettuce. In the evening, we had fish soup, the *crustaces* fished off Corsica and tinned on the Continent, with Corsican *vin rosé* and lots of it — not for the effect, he claimed, but for *la soif*.

On Corsica you never wear a tie. You put espadrilles on your feet. Tim's walking consisted of circling the local *supermarché* with a trolley every day. He never frequented cafés, except once a week, when he had a standing date with an English couple for a Dutch dinner. The four of us met in the Trou, a café on the port, and then went on to a restaurant. Everyone ordered the menu. The three indulged in local gossip. All I had to do was to go on eating. The wife, Lady Tartempion, wore a spotless, sleeveless, white dress; her arms were freckled. She had just come from the hairdresser, where she went regularly, driving miles into the mountains to return with a Mrs Thatcher look. She resembled that lady in other ways, being energetic, vivacious and a forceful talker. On her third glass of *rosé*, she turned to me.

'You were married to Cyril Connolly?'

'Yes.'

'What a dreadful man. We used to see a lot of him on the Brains Trust.'

'Really?'

'Oh yes. Every week. He never said much, but looked thoroughly disagreeable with food all over his waistcoat. Conceited, too.'

'He wasn't, you know.'

'Well, he was very ugly, you can't deny that.' The attack went on, with me parrying, until she suddenly snapped. 'Why are you defending him? You left him, didn't you?'

A few days later, Tim drove me into the country. We had been invited up to their English pre-fab, which looked rather incongruous plonked in a Corsican gully: posh bathrooms, gleaming knobs, clinical atmosphere. While drinking Moët et Chandon on the terrace, we admired the bleak, blue swimming pool. The husband had left us to sit in his caravan.

'He often sleeps in it', she said, 'with his ham radio going, tuned into people all over the world.' They mentioned another 'Lady' on the fringe of the English contingent. I said I would like to meet her. 'She couldn't stand Cyril. He snubbed her once throughout an entire luncheon. She wouldn't fancy meeting you.'

As we left, Lady Tartempion said, suspiciously, 'Staying long?'

I asked Tim if he found her attractive.

'Well, she does take care of herself and, when she goes to England, she often gets picked up on the boat. Does anyone ever pick you up?'

From then on, should either of the 'Ladies' get a mention, I referred to them as the 'Dead-Men Haters' and the atmosphere chilled, though Tim went on being a good host, creeping down the stairs so as not to disturb me; or was it the espadrilles which gave that impression? He was prompt at swishing a letter under my door, forthcoming about changing a forty-watt bulb for one I could read by, and good at providing clean sheets and towels, pretty ones too, from Peter Jones, when a note would be left in the hall: 'Laundry swap for HELP am tomorrow.' All this had an odd effect. I, too, crept about in espadrilles, hid behind doors, scuttled away at the sound of footsteps, whispered to Suki and every morning, at the precise hour of 10.30, peeped through the lavatory slats to watch Tim get into his Fiat, rev the engine, reverse and drive very carefully down the vertical hill to his *supermarché*. Then I relaxed and dressed and, leaving Suki stretched out like a sphinx on the veranda, walked by a devious route to the same market and climbed up again lugging cat food. Then I fled for the day, when a great weight of sadness lifted, to lie on the sands and read *Tribune*. Should we meet simultaneously at the front door, Tim would smile, and say, 'About to take your walk? You'll find it hot.' I, too, left notes: 'Ants climbing the drainpipe, heading for the watch tower,' and the next time we clashed on the porch he said, 'I'm grateful to you for telling me that.' We even got together, heads down, trying to follow their trail.

Along the Cours Napoléon there is a constant *embouteillage* and no parking space. Sitting in one of the cafés on the Cours Grandval, where a stream of traffic roared past, a treat of the day might be an icecream.

'*Trois boules. Vanille, praline et fraise, sans crème, s'il vous plaît.*'

Pack-laden girls plodded by in a temperature of ninety degrees and one saw a certain amount of provincial chic, women with unshaven armpits and false pearls, dressed entirely in black with husbands in cheap tan suits. There were excursions into the *maquis*. To Bonifacio. Sarthène. Cargèse. These tours were supposed to be gay; the drivers were pale, fat and black-chested, with sex appeal. The radio droned out sad, sentimental music; while turning a hairpin bend, the driver would grab the mike and give interesting information on the scenery, another *chène liège*, or 'There's a myrtle. Olives. See?' Or else he'd joke.

'*Pourquoi Napoléon n'a pas attaché son cheval à un arbre?*' He'd regard us through the windscreen mirror and, undaunted, continue, '*Parce que les Corses ne sont pas les sandwiches.*'

Trying on shoes on the Cours Napoléon, the salesgirl was very young and particularly agreeable. Nowadays, sales ladies are inclined to snap so. She even took the precaution of making sure the sandals fitted. They were hectic pink and she said, '*Ce n'est pas trop vilain comme couleur?*' Pleased with the transaction, I asked if she would mind throwing away my smelly espadrilles; she laughed and said excitedly, 'Are you English?'

'Yes, but I live in France.' (After living in a country for fifteen years, it's irksome to be taken for a tourist.)

---

* Dorothy Carrington wrote *Granite Island*, a now classic account of the history and civilisation of Corsica.

'You remind me so much of Lady Carrington. Dorety.* Do you know her?' The salesgirl beamed and her praise of Dorety was ardent. '*Elle est si sympa,*' she repeated. Had I heard of Dorothy? From Tim. *Bien sûr*. He had mentioned having had to pick her up once at the airport, and wow! the number of suitcases; and how, during her visit to England, he had climbed up on to the hot little terrace of her apartment every day to water the plants. And one didn't have to inquire whether or not he'd been 'put owt' by it.

Thinking it might amuse him, I repeated the *sympa* story.

'You don't look at all like her, you know.' His tone was very grave, confirming what I had already suspected. The salesgirl had been paying me a nice compliment. How agreeable it would have been to have met Dorothy; at this stage, almost anybody would have done. 'She never took to Cyril, you know.' Tim's tone was vehement.

Still, Corsica had not lost all its charm. Old church bells still chimed. The people remained quite friendly – Corsican people, that is. The *charcuterie* was good; the *confit de chataigne* and tomatoes were delicious. And there would always be Tino Rossi.

One wonders sometimes what goes on behind the scenes in restaurants. In Corsica you don't have to look that far. Dining alone in Ajaccio, a cockroach actually ran across the plate and, in spite of several attacks with a napkin, got away, taking my appetite with it.

Chapter XXI

Adieu, Poules

They fuck you up your Mum and Dad. They may not mean to, but they do.
They fill you with the faults they had and add some extra, just for you.

'This Be the Verse', Philip Larkin

I cannot terminate these memoirs without relating the bane of my life – teeth – having inherited dental trouble from poor Mummy who, to cure chronic indigestion, at the age of forty had all her uppers pulled out by Mr Pain. In order to avoid a similar fate, I have run through almost as many dentists as lovers.

In France, I have been to several more. There, if you owe money, it is not the secretary who presses you to pay, but the dentist himself, who follows you out shouting abuse, or his wife waylays you with a bill while looking pointedly at any jewellery pinned to your suit. Added to which, most dentists in France are considered to be millionaires. Mr Santanelli, of Italian origin, had a superb waiting room overlooking the sea in St Tropez. The first time I went to him I had no money on me. Although I had made a further appointment, he confiscated my emerald ring while I walked across to a bank. The next dentist was a Spaniard who had a reputation for being the best parodontologist on the coast. He practised in an apartment overlooking the sea in Menton, where I would drive twice a week, a journey of two hours or more each way. His remedy for bleeding gums was to burn them, medieval fashion, with a poker-like instrument. I then consulted Mr Meyer, who held court in even more sumptuous surroundings overlooking the sea, not far from the Carlton in Cannes. He had also been trained in the States. Bernard came with me and, after our painful treatment, we were both handed treble whiskies which went down tenfold on my bill. Bernard got away without ever paying.

Mitterrand was about to be elected President. Assuming the country had gone communist, Meyer fled to Texas. I then became resigned to being treated by an Algerian in Cogolin. But he never pleaded for money; instead, as

159

I lived so near, he sent a threatening emissary up to the *mas*. By this time, so much had been spent on dentistry that I had hardly any money left over to eat. So I fled to Recloses to stay with François Michel. When he saw how the Algerian had treated my teeth, he said it looked as though I had the same dentist as Queen Elizabeth of England. Whereupon Bernard was instantly loyal – one of the rare occasions when he was. He said to François, who had no teeth at all and was always leaving his false set on the dining table, that he looked as though he had the same dentist as Malraux, whom everyone knew had no teeth left either.

I then went to a Paris dentist who had been recommended by Meyer. Altmayer respected Meyer and thought he would regret fleeing the country to become a 'big frog in a tiny Texas pool'. The walls of the inner sanctum of Altmayer's quarters on the Avenue Montaigne were covered with signed photographs of celebrities. If I wanted to impress, I told people that I had the same dentist as the President. But even multimillionaires like to be paid.

Whereas in our hey-day, as soon as he awoke, Bernard would come up to my room and inquire how I'd slept, on his last visit, after hauling in four suitcases, he said, 'I suppose you know why I'm here. I've come to finish my book.' And from then on he only mounted the stairs to prepare the spare room for his mother, who arrived a month later. Sometimes when I went down to prepare my breakfast, I was likely to find this kind of thing propped over the sink:

> Dear Little Madame Gaylord-Hauser, If Bernard Shaw lived to such a great age (he died short of 100) it wasn't because, as you think, he didn't eat meat but because he hardly ever made love and because he had great contempt for *qui vous sert de tête*. PS Very happy to have instructed you on such a point of detail. *Le Pic de la Miraudole*.

Since then I have been told that even in this day and age, Maigret, Simenon's hero, always addresses his wife courteously as 'Madame'; in France, with some couples, the closer the relationship, the more formal the address. However, I was never particularly flattered should Bernard, disturbed by my stacking, enter the kitchen and exclaim, '*Oh, c'est VOUS!* I thought it was the cat.' And he didn't mean Mell or Suki, but the black Tom that used to haunt the terrace, depositing *crottes*.

In the final months at the *mas*, evenings were very sad. While Bernard worked out an endgame of chess that he followed in *Le Monde*, I played solitaire. So I was surprised and flattered when reading *Un Siècle Débordé* to come upon this:

La Retraite à Quarante Ans: Aux bords de la quarantaine je quittai Paris pour un couvent près de Grimaud dont la mère supérieure était une anglaise d'une grande beauté qui m'apprit la frugalité, les vertus du silence et le plaisir, partagé avec des fouines et des renards, d'avoir des poules. Et forcément je me remis à écrire; aurais-je fait d'autre?*

— implying that our puritan existence had suited him. During the last month, his mother fell ill and when she came out of hospital, rather than remain in Paris, we thought she might prefer to convalesce in the Midi. Bernard prepared her room with great care, laying down a rug. And I went to pick her up at St Raphael. Madame Frank did not seem to be at all frail. She ate well, took short walks, until one afternoon she disappeared for hours, having got lost in the forest, and was brought back by a stranger. Then suddenly she fell ill again and I drove her into the clinic, where she underwent an operation. Bernard visited his mother every day. Either I would drive him in or he ordered a taxi. We were both getting on so badly that I did not behave as well as I should and the circumstances of her sudden death in the middle of the night, when neither of us heard the telephone, even now can instil a feeling of guilt.

During his various sojourns at the *mas*, Bernard wrote two books. In 1971, *Un Siècle Débordé* won the Deux Magots literary award. Ten years later, *Solde* was inscribed, '*Pour Barbara avec toute ma tendresse passée, présente et future,*' and the last passage reads:

La maison proche de Grimaud où ma mère a passé en Mai 1979 ses dernières vacances a été vendue. Je n'ai plus rien à faire ici. Je vous laisse. Quand vous aurez terminé votre lecture, n'oubliez pas à d'éteindre les lumières en partant.†

The day after his mother's death, Bernard was packed and ready to leave. '*Pauvre petite Maman*' were almost his final words. A taxi filled with suitcases awaited him in the drive, when he followed me up the hill, where I had gone to feed the *poules*. Closing the gate of the cage that had once housed the poor coatis, he turned and said, quietly, '*Adieu, poules, et merci*', which must have included me. It was the last of him. A year later, I happened to run into him at

---

* Retirement at Forty: Approaching the age of forty I left Paris for a convent near Grimaud, where the Mother Superior was an English woman of great beauty who taught me frugality, the virtues of silence and the pleasure, shared with ferrets and foxes, of going after chickens. And inevitably I started writing again; would I have done otherwise?

† The house near Grimaud where my mother spent her last holiday in May 1979 has been sold. There's nothing more for me to do here. I leave you. When you have finished reading, don't forget to turn out the lights before going.

a dinner given by the artists Claude and François Lalanne, and he made a telling remark,

'I am now the same age you were when I first knew you. Don't you think you were lucky to have had such a *jeune garçon* as a lover all those years?'

And Bernard Frank went on holding forth to a roomful of people while I stumbled in the dark to the car and drove sadly home.

Index

Spender, Stephen, 14, 76, 83, 108
Sprague, Jane, 89
Stein, Jean, 50
Sutro, John, 6, 15, 18, 23, 60–2, 65–7, 70, 80, 83

Taki, 103
Thérèse, servant at *mas*, 126–7, 136, 138, 143–4, 152
Thompson, Gogi and Lee, 66
Toot, 82
Topolski, Feliks, 6, 17, 23, 45, 49, 50
Treat, Roger, 81, 84–5, 95
Trilling, Lionel, 86
Tunnard, Peter, 60
Turner, Chuck, 83, 93
Tynan, Elaine, 68, 83–4
Tynan, Kenneth, 53, 55, 67–8, 83–4

Vadim, Roger, 151
Volpi, Countess, 1

Warhol, Andy, 112–3
Watson, Peter, 10, 14
Weidenfeld, George, 1–9, 11, 12, 15–19, 21, 23, 25–9, 33–4, 37–9, 41, 43–62; marriage to author, 48; 60–2, 64, 66–7, 70–1; divorce, 88; 103–4, 110, 115, 117, 132
Weldon, Angelica, 63
Westoff, Bob, 143
Wilson, Angus, 12, 47
Wilson, Mr and Mrs Edmund, 86
Windsor, the Duke and Duchess of, 115
Wishart, Michael, 68–9, 71–2, 74, 76–7, 88
Wong, Anna May, 12

Young, Gavin, 102–3, 116